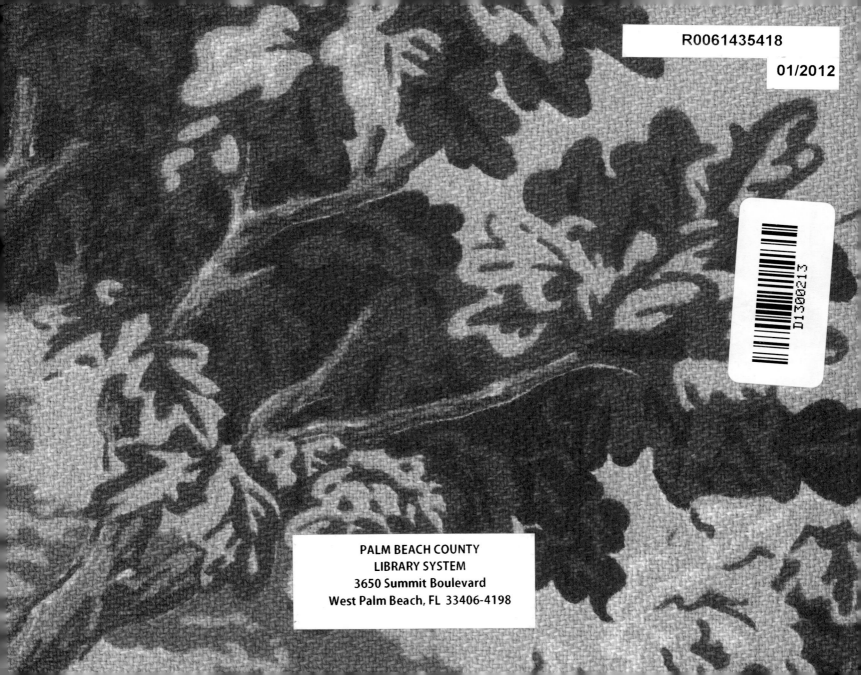

A VERY MODEST COTTAGE

A **COUNTRY LIVING** Book

A VERY MODEST COTTAGE

Tereasa Surratt

HEARST BOOKS
A division of Sterling Publishing Co., Inc.

New York / London
www.sterlingpublishing.com

Log Cabin Tourist Camp.
½ Mile East of Bluff Springs
Route 67

Guest Log

CONTENTS

"*I would rather be shut up in a very modest cottage with my books, my family, and a few old friends, dining on simple bacon and letting the world roll on as it liked, than to occupy the most splendid post, which any human power can give.*"

THOMAS JEFFERSON,
THIRD PRESIDENT OF
THE UNITED STATES

INTRODUCTION

From the day we decided to move and restore the cabin to the night that that we pounded the last nail was only three short months. But the journey of discovery that unfolded afterwards has been three years and running. We could not have guessed how many stories the little cabin would reveal to us over time.

I'd grown up with this cabin. It sat next to my grandmother's house my entire life in the small farming community of Beardstown, Illinois. If you happened past it just a few years ago, you probably would have agreed that it had long since outlived its usefulness. But I believe when you have an emotional attachment to something, it can never be too far gone. I was six years old when I first saw the cabin and told my dad I planned on "moving in and making it my house." He agreed nothing was beyond fixing, even that abandoned wreck. He always believed the door to possibility never really closes, and because he instilled that belief in me, that little cabin now enjoys a new life as a beloved yet modest haven for us in Sugar Creek, Wisconsin.

I like to think a bit of the collective good energy of all the souls who have passed through its door still lives and breathes inside and that every guest who spends a night adds a bit more good karma to a cabin that will continue to live and breathe long after me. I know my dad would agree. Thank you, Dad. This book is for you.

—*Tereasa Surratt*

LEFT: *The author takes a break on the front steps of the cottage.*

Chapter One

LOST AND FOUND

I had been dreaming about the cabin ever since I was knee-high to a grasshopper (as Dad would say). It sat next to Grandma's house for five straight decades, with three generations of us—starting with Grandma when she was a girl—daydreaming about growing up and making it *our* house. It was, after all, child size in its 12-foot-by-12-foot glory.

SAVING A LOST SOUL

I have always thought, even at six years old, that the little cabin seemed sad. Why didn't somebody paint it? Didn't it have a family? Where did the bed go? Why did there always seem to be a nest

They said I was crazy. At times, I thought they might be right.

of wasps inside? So, thirty years later, I finally came to the conclusion that the cabin was waiting to be rescued. It had hung on all this time, making it through harsh Midwestern winters, yearning for the day that somebody would see past its run-down exterior, and say "Hey, I'll bet she'd clean up real nice!"

That somebody turned out to be me. And that was the beginning of saving a piece of forgotten Americana, transporting a piece of my hometown in Illinois across one state line to my new home in Wisconsin, and restoring a little cabin to make it the house I'd dreamed of as a kid. The best lesson I learned is that it's never too late.

OPPOSITE: *If you stood in the center of the abandoned cabin and listened closely, you might have been able to hear it whisper, "I used to be cute. I had visitors all the time. I'm just a little rough around the edges—nothing a little elbow grease can't fix!" At least that's what I heard.*

LEFT: *The remains of the hopeful cabin's front door.*

Tourist Park, Ontonagon, Mich. — M-778

Tourist cabins like these were popular in the 1920s. They all had the same things in common: modesty, simplicity, and functionality.

HUMBLE BEGINNINGS

Back in the early 1920s, if you wanted to hit the road either for work or play, where would you spend the night? In today's world of GPS systems, smart phones, and turn-by-turn directions, it's easy to forget that it wasn't until 1925 that the federal government instituted a national road numbering system made up of standardized routes and road signs. All of a sudden, traveling by car became a whole lot easier. Motor clubs like the Automobile Association of America distributed road maps listing roadside lodging. The age of the driving vacation had begun.

The choice of lodging for transient travelers back then ranged from fancy hotels in town (expensive) right down to "travel camps," which were basically large grassy areas. For a small fee, the travel camp owners offered a place to park your car and pitch a tent. Some even provided public toilets and showers.

By 1922 the U.S. Chamber of Commerce estimated that more than one thousand free tourist tenting camps for transient travelers had been built from coast to coast, funded by the states to promote tourism. As more cars started to hit the road, entrepising farmers and landowners began erecting modest, homemade cabins on their land and renting them to travelers for minimal nightly fees. The first of this crop was typically only one step above camping out but offered more privacy and the convenience of not having to set up a tent.

13

Camp owners quickly realized that offering customers accommodations in the form of cabins instead of tents meant profits all year round, rather than just in the warm summer vacationing months. Their competition for tourist customers who wanted better accommodations than commercial travelers and were willing to pay for it led to fanciful architectural gimmicks: faux teepees, Spanish villas, and log cabins started replacing the standard, generic cabins. The era of roadside tent camping fell by the wayside, and the term *cabin camp* was officially born.

By the end of the decade, the cabin camp evolved to the cabin court—a less unsavory name, given the reputation the orginal tent camps had of attracting undesirable crowds such as Depression-era hobos and small-time criminals. Cabin courts were also called motor hotels, which later would be abbreviated to *motels*. In the late 1920s, our own little cabin was part of a family of four log cabins competing for guests along Route 125 in Beardstown, Illinois, in the heart of "Lincoln Land," making its log cabin theme perfectly logical.

BELOW: *Postcards advertising a camp's features, such as "entertaining stages," would draw customers.*

OPPOSITE: *This cabin's style is similar to ours—simple, modest, functional, and tiny!*

CABIN — BIRCHWOOD RESORT, WALKER, MINN.

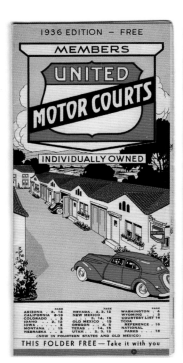

THE RUSTIC THEATER AT THE UNDERWOOD MOTOR CAMP

The cabin's eventual fate is a familiar story. Like so many other small towns, ours was eventually bypassed by a bigger, better highway, which was built in the 1920s. With the main artery of commerce now leading elsewhere, local businesses gradually dried up. Our little cabin, along with its brothers and sisters who sat eagerly alongside the highway, doors open and ready to take in weary travelers, had worn out its usefulness and now sat silently, entering into a slow decline.

ABOVE: *Brochures listing tourist camps, like these examples from the 1920s, remained popular promotions through the 1930s and 1940s.*

Camps of CRIME

by *J. Edgar Hoover*
WITH COURTNEY RYLEY COOPER

by *J. Edgar Hoover*
WITH COURTNEY RYLEY COOPER

Behind many alluring roadside signs are dens of vice and corruption, says America's head G-Man ... He points out

SURVEYING THE DAMAGE

It was easy to imagine Bonnie and Clyde–style roadside travelers camping out for a night in our cabin. Or even a happy family of four on their way to a summertime fishing trip. Smitten with visions of bringing it back from the brink, I started making plans. But there was the reality of logistics to consider. How exactly does one move an entire building (albeit a tiny one) across two states? You don't. You bribe your little brother into doing it. A MacGyver of all things mechanical, I knew Sam would step up to the challenge. Of course, he told me I was nuts right away. But once he eventually agreed, he started sketching plans on a napkin. "First," he said, "we have to see what we've got to work with." He was referring to the fifty years of deferred maintenance and floor-to-ceiling junk pile that had accumulated inside.

The cabin was a shadow of its former self. A ghost of a once bustling, proud and accommodating shelter, it sat with its sister cabins, ever ready and waiting for tourists during the Roaring Twenties.

Before we could even think about moving the cabin, we first had to empty it out, survey the damage, make some repairs, and get it stablized. This is what we discovered: Roof shingles: missing. Electrical: mouse-chewed. Log siding: rotting. Upon inspection, it was clear that there was a lot of work ahead of us. But with only a single room—no kitchen or bath—I thought the cabin would be relatively easy to restore. *With no plumbing, it would be easier to restore—right?*

ABOVE, LEFT *(Clockwise from top right): The paint was peeling, windows broken, the door a flaking mess, and the interior piled high with debris. She was a sad sight.*

ABOVE, RIGHT: *The cabin sat in Beardstown, Illinois, alongside her twin sister. Our cabin is on the right. Note the missing shingles.*

RIGHT: *A detail of the extent of the peeling paint on the exterior.*

"It doesn't look too far gone to me—nothing a little elbow grease can't fix."

TOM SURRATT, MY DAD

UNCOVERING THE BONES

LEFT: *Meet the cleaner—my brother Sam—gutting the guts. Never one to fear hard labor, he just threw gloves at me and told me to "grab an end." He remembers the cabin as a kid as well—especially how fascinated he was with all the junk inside.*

Two dumpsters and six hours later, we unearthed the guts. Under a tangled pile of tomato cages, we found a couple of apple crates, a folding wooden chair, and a few cigar boxes that were salvagable. Eventually, the bones started to reveal themselves. Wow. There was a floor! And an early electrical heater that appeared to have been installed in the thirties, judging by its post–art deco design.

We also found some things that we hesitated to study too closely. I couldn't quite tell how long that rodent had been dead, but its skeletal remains indicated the better part of a year. No glass in the windows—all the better to see in the plain light of day exactly what I'd gotten myself into.

HOW TO LOAD A CABIN ONTO A HUMONGOUS TRAILER

1. Set aside 10 hours to prep the cabin for hoisting.

2. Remove excess glass.

3. Brace the interior floor with boards (to minimize flex).

4. Tie-down strap the exterior walls to stablize and support.

5. Scoop it up with a Bobcat (using a fork attachment).

6. Lower it onto a trailer and tie it down.

7. Board up the windows with plywood.

READY...SET...HEAVE!

Luckily for us, the cabin sat on the grounds of a truckyard, meaning that Sam had access to cranes, Bobcats, trailers, jacks—pretty much everything we needed. After some serious planning and a lot of elbow grease, he managed to hoist the cabin onto the trailer. With the cabin loaded up and strapped down, she waited on her trailer overnight, ready for the journey early the following morning.

"Ten dollars says it'll fall apart before you hit Route 55," said our friends—ever the optimists. But we'd come this far; there was no turning back now.

OPPOSITE: *The cabin crouching under one of the truckyard cranes.*

LEFT: *The cabin, snuggling in for its trip through the dozens of towns on the way from Beardstown, Illinois, to Elkhorn, Wisconsin.*

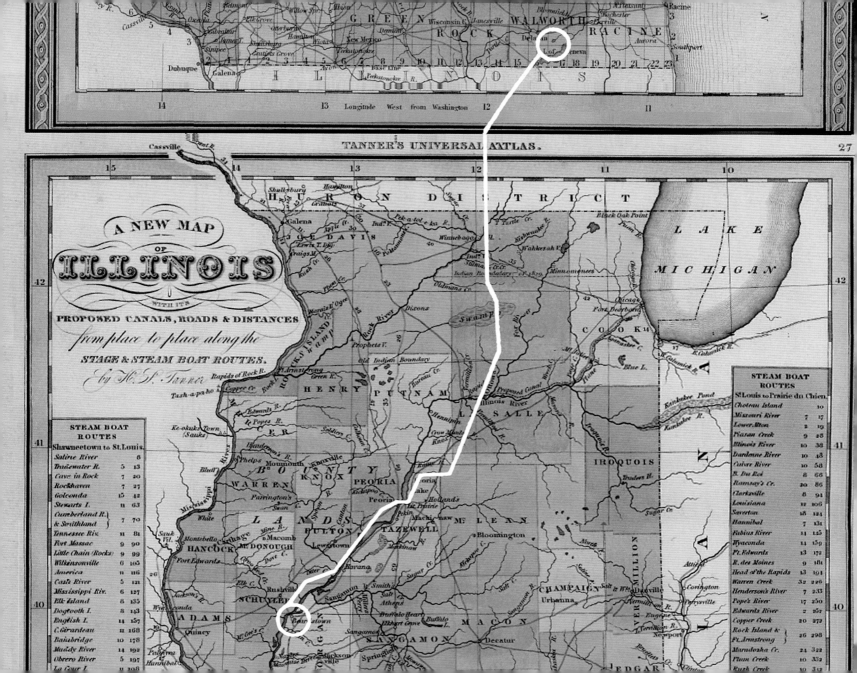

A NEW MAP OF ILLINOIS

WITH ITS
PROPOSED CANALS, ROADS & DISTANCES
from place to place along the
STAGE & STEAM BOAT ROUTES.
By H. S. Tanner

STEAM BOAT ROUTES Shawneetown to St. Louis.		
Saline River		6
Tradewater R.	5	13
Cave in Rock	7	20
Rockhaven	7	27
Golconda	15	42
Stewarts I.	13	63
Cumberland R. & Smithland	7	70
Tennessee Riv.	11	81
Fort Massac	9	90
Little Chain (Rocks)	9	99
Wilkinsonville	6	105
America	11	116
Cash River	5	121
Mississippi Riv.	6	127
Elk Island	8	135
Dogtooth I.	8	143
English I.	14	157
C. Girardeau	11	168
Bainbridge	10	178
Muddy River	14	192
Obrero River	5	197
La Cour I.	11	208

STEAM BOAT ROUTES St. Louis to Prairie du Chien.		
Choteau Island		10
Missouri River	7	17
Lower Alton	2	19
Piasau Creek	9	28
Illinois River	10	38
Darlene River	10	48
Culver River	10	58
S. Du Roi	8	66
Ramsey's Cr.	20	86
Clarksville	8	94
Louisiana	12	106
Saverton	18	124
Hannibal	1	125
Fabius River	11	125
Wyaconda	11	159
Ft. Edwards	13	172
R. des Moines	9	181
Head of the Rapids	13	191
Warren Creek	32	226
Henderson's River	7	233
Popes River	17	250
Edwards River	7	257
Copper Creek	20	272
Rock Island & Ft. Armstrong	26	298
Marudoska Cr.	24	322
Plum Creek	10	332
Rush Creek	10	342

Chapter Two

POTENTIAL ON WHEELS

Now that the cabin was cleaned up, loaded up, and strapped down, it was time to hit the road. It would be a long haul from Beardstown, Illinois (the Land of Lincoln) to Elkhorn, Wisconsin (America's Dairyland). So on provisions and a prayer, we took to the farm roads on a journey to a new home.

FACT: MANUAL LABOR IS ALWAYS EASIER AFTER DINER CHOW

I had used all of my powers of persuasion, including my specialty—homemade cookies alternated with sisterly guilt trips—to convince my brother to move the cabin for me. Move it across two states, over the river, and through the woods. And over bridges. And around roadblocks. Move it 245 miles from its birthplace in Beardstown, Illinois (Land of Lincoln), to Elkhorn, Wisconsin (America's Dairyland). I'd persuaded my husband, David, to join the party, too.

The magical powers of caffeine are key when tackling a project as massive as this. Eggs and bacon help, too. So my truckers started the big day at the Star Café. It's the Times Square of Beardstown, as it's always jam packed in the morning. Everybody knows you whether they know you or not, and you are always welcomed with a smile and a cup of coffee. The beautiful thing about pulling up to a stool at this diner (and most hometown cafés like it) is that there is no shortage of advice to be had. Plus, farmers have the best tips about anything related to machinery and the art of hauling. Running farms makes them by necessity jacks of all trades. The farmers in Beardstown are just all-round good guys who are a pleasure to keep company with. So if you get to belly up next to one, do it. You are sure to learn something.

OPPOSITE: *Sam (center) and David, my husband, (right) started out at the Star Café in Beardstown, where coffee, smiles, and great advice are served fresh daily.*

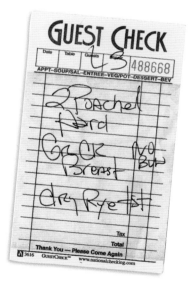

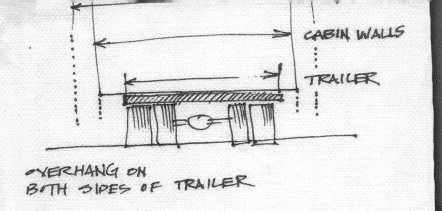

CABIN WALLS

TRAILER

OVERHANG ON
BOTH SIDES OF TRAILER

SAMANTHA

WELCOME

DIXIE TRAVEL PLAZA
I55 & US136   IL
MCLEAN

280625230010001
VISA
INVOICE# 007827

PUMP # 07
PRODUCT: PREM
GALLONS: 14.466
PRICE/G: $ 1.879
FUEL SALE $ 27.18
AUTH# 028363
****CHARGE****

THANK YOU
HAVE A NICE DAY

It turns out that when you want to move a building across a state line, you need two of everything. Two permits. Two drivers. Two maps. Two CB radios. A double dose of patience. And a good sense of humor. (The entertainment value of CB slang cannot be underestimated on long hauls.) It also doesn't hurt to be the gambling type. The risk factor: How many miles could one travel before a 50-mile-per-hour wind force would blow apart an eighty-five-year-old building? Needless to say, it was a long, tedious, and worrisome trip.

When you apply for a hauling permit, the state generates a driving map for you that is appropriate for the height, width, and weight of your load. At least that takes the guessing out of, *Can our load fit under this overpass?* and, *Can we get across this bridge without it caving in on us?* We've all learned a lesson by example when driving past an unlucky trucker stuck under an low bridge. Not pretty.

OPPOSITE: *The smartest thinking is sometimes best executed on a napkin. So many things to consider, not the least of which was how much overhang was possible (and legal). Luckily, we overestimated the width of the cabin when sketching, and it wasn't a problem.*

LEFT: *We were so well prepared, it was almost disappointing not to be stopped by a trooper to show off our hauling permit.*

ON THE ROAD AGAIN

The moment of truth had arrived. We were ready to hit the road. Uneasiness started to set in. Would it slide off the back? Bounce off the trailer? I couldn't shake from my mind images of chunks of roofing and siding flying onto other travelers' windshields, wildlife running for cover. The fact that I was stuck in Prague on a business trip didn't make things any easier. I was on the phone with my husband (who was in the "leader truck") every 20 minutes. In the end, it all came down to calculating risk. The more uncertain they were about the conditions of the road and the weather, the slower they would drive. If that meant a crawling speed of 25 mph, then that was the accepted fate. After all, nobody wanted to see the roof scraped away after underestimating bridge clearance, or a wheel coming off after taking a corner too fast. We'd resigned ourselves to the trip taking a minimum of 15 hours. (Under normal circumstances, it's a 6-hour drive. It ended up taking 10.) That's the beauty of low expectations. You are never disappointed if you predict only disaster. After all, the weather forecast did call for rain. And so it went, with me calling at 2:00 AM Czech time, then 2:20, and 2:40, and so on...until they stopped picking up my calls. I can't say as I blame them. But I didn't get any sleep.

ABOVE: *Our hauler and leader vehicles. The leader blocked the bridges, watched for falling tie-down straps, and alerted us to roadblocks and hazards. Thank God we had both.*

RIGHT: *At 15 miles per gallon, the team made five stops to refuel.*

WELCOME TO
WISCONSIN

I was right to worry. Other things to consider when pulling a wide load: narrow lanes, blind corners, other wide loads coming in the opposite direction—look out for the tractor!—and lots and lots of gas money. The walkie-talkies were priceless when it was time for the lead vehicle and hauling vehicle to communicate for stops, potential road hazards, and the errant pet in the road. Also necessary: a folder with your permits, license, and insurance at the ready in case you get pulled over.

LEFT: *Some of the views from behind the hauler. Pit stops along the way were frequent and necessary.*

WHAT IS A "BRIDGE HIT"?

When you get stuck trying to drive under a low bridge. (They call it "bridge bashing" in the UK.)

HOW YOU GET YOURSELF INTO ONE

A simple miscalculation of your vehicle's height. And sometimes when the road (unbeknownst to the driver) rises a few inches, which can make all the difference.

HOW YOU GET YOURSELF OUT OF ONE

Let the air out of your tires, dropping your height enough to squeeze yourself out.

HOW OFTEN DO PEOPLE FIND THEM-SELVES STUCK?

Recently, in New Jersey alone, New Jersey Transit said its railroad bridges were struck 135 times in the course of a year.

HOW TO INCREASE YOUR ODDS OF AVOIDING ONE

The *McNally Motor Carrier Atlas* is the bible of safety, listing bridge clearances and restricted routes that trucks cannot go on or under.

As my brother and husband drove past abandoned buildings while making their way to Wisconsin, these sad structures seemed to stare mournfully at the little house we'd rescued from their own certain fate.

A LITTLE TO THE LEFT.... STOP!

Where once sat a tired-out Airstream (that we donated to restorers) marked the spot for the new cabin footprint—a perch overlooking a little lake called Wandawega in Elkhorn, Wisconsin. Exhausted from the long trip, covered in mud, and drenched from the incessant rain, my brother Sam wrestled the cabin off the trailer in the downpour. This meant bringing in an ever-so-versatile Bobcat, using the front-loader attachment to lift the massive branches hovering above the cabin just enough to let us move in. He had to back the trailer into the exact spot where the cabin would sit, which meant that the entire load had to be wedged between two large trees. With mere inches on either side and above, a collective sigh of relief could be heard once the trailer was squeezed in. Next would come several hours during which Sam and David manhandled it with a fork truck, hand jack, and a few logs to nestle it into its new woodsy nest.

RIGHT: *Upon arrival at the lake, they had to take it very slow as they backed carefully into position (bottom four images). It was tricky to get the cabin under the power lines and down the entrance (top left), under low tree branches (center left) and around tight corners (large image).*

WANDAWEGA
LAKE RESORT
W5453

WIDE LOAD

With the trailer backed into the precise spot, they put a house jack on one side of the cabin to lift it up a few inches off the trailer, then stabilized the corners with stacks of tree stumps. Then they went to the opposite side, also lifting it a few

We were halfway home.

inches and shoving more tree stumps underneath. Now they had the little cabin jacked up on tree stumps, hovering— teetering—precariously above the trailer. They ever so carefully pulled the trailer out, leaving the cabin suspended a few feet in the air, trailer gone from beneath it. Then we set the corner cinder blocks underneath the cabin (and only then did it stop raining) and lowered the cabin one side at a time, four inches at a time, by removing the tree stumps and lowering the house jack. It became official at that moment. The little cabin was successfully transformed from a roadside motorlodge cabin into a lakeside cabin. We were halfway home.

OPPOSITE: *My brother, Sam, slowly lowers the cabin onto its foundation of cinder blocks (from left to right top row):*

1: Setting with Bobcat

2: Sliding in stumps for support

3: Replacing stumps with blocks

4: Leveling with hand jack

5: "Lifting" the cabin

6: Setting center blocks

LEFT: *She was safely and squarely in her new home, where she will be for the rest of her days.*

41

WHY THE CABIN CALLS WISCONSIN HOME

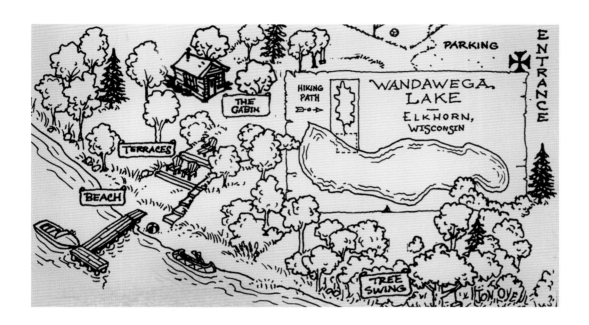

LEFT: *A hand-rendered map of the property, showing where the cabin sits on the grounds.*

FAR LEFT: *Scenes from our camp at Lake Wandawega.*

OVERLEAF: *The new view from the cabin's back door.*

Why Wisconsin? How did this little slice of my small-town Illinois childhood end up in Wisconsin? As it turns out, I'm not the only member of my family interested in preserving pieces of my past. My husband David had a similar dream, on a slightly larger scale. The cabin's new home, the historic Wandawega Lake Resort, was David's family getaway from the 1960s through the 1980s. This once run-down lake lodge is not only the home of our modest cottage, it's now the subject of a seemingly never-ending, full-scale, family camp renovation project!

When you have only 121 square feet, it's nice to have a room with a view.

Chapter Three

HOPE AND A HAMMER

With the little cottage now nestled in its perch over the lake, it was time to strap on our toolbelts. We thought the hardest part was behind us. We had, after all, made it 245 miles on country roads and highways through a rainstorm, and remained intact. Little did we know the job that lay ahead.

MOM ALWAYS SAID:

FAILING TO PLAN IS PLANNING TO FAIL

Which means I've got a lot of homework ahead. Where in the world are we going to find half-log tongue-and-groove drop siding, circa 1920, to match the exterior? If I put a potbelly stove in that corner, how long will it take to fall through the floor? Should we evict that family of squirrels squatting in the attic, or can we learn to cohabitate? All good questions.

This was going to require a lot of shopping. Thank God I am gifted in *that* department. Thinking I might as well tackle the big stuff first, I started with a trip to the local lumberyard. I took some photos and a rotted chunk of the half sawn log siding with me and offered it up for inspection, explaining my dilemma. When the proprietor saw my pictures she said, "Oh, honey. It looks like you're gonna need a lot more than some drop siding." She was right, of course. But you have to start somewhere. And by the grace of the DIY gods, the lumberyard just happened to have a specialty source to get the right wood, so we ordered it right away. The day my shipment arrived was like Christmas. There it was on the back of the lumberyard fork truck pallet: the first little bit of light at the end of the rehab tunnel had started to show in the form of half sawn logs.

RIGHT: *I am, admittedly a compulsive listmaker. Here are just a few of my many pages of sketches and plans. I started with a list for contents, then ended up making lists for measurements to make sure they would all fit. I even made lists for color combination options.*

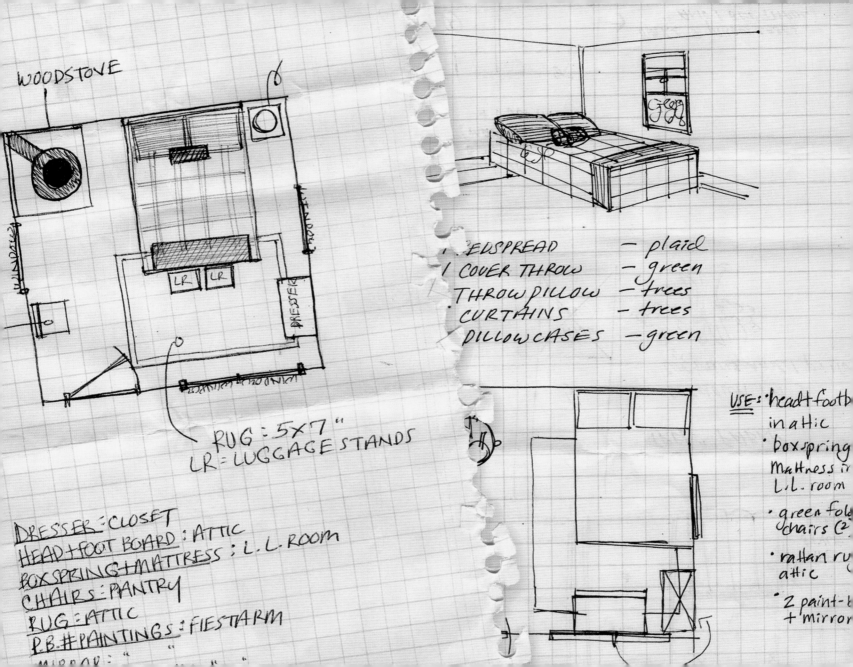

WOODSTOVE

RUG: 5X7"
LR = LUGGAGE STANDS

DRESSER = CLOSET
HEAD + FOOT BOARD : ATTIC
BOXSPRING + MATTRESS : L.L. ROOM
CHAIRS : PANTRY
RUG : ATTIC
P.B. # PAINTINGS : FIESTA RM
MIRROR : "

BEDSPREAD — plaid
COVER THROW — green
THROW PILLOW — trees
CURTAINS — trees
PILLOWCASES — green

USE: head+foot b
in attic
• box spring
mattress i
L.L. room
• green fol
chairs (2
• rattan ru
attic
• 2 paint-b
+ mirror

If you stood in front of the cabin and squinted your eyes, you could see…its younger self. The cabin had been waiting a long time—nearly eighty years—to become once again the guest cabin it was intended to be. The photo overlay shown here demonstrates what I saw in my mind's eye—the "after."

IT'S HERE! NOW WHAT?

And so it began: the real work. Our to-do list was a mile long. We needed to fix the windows, rebuild the door, install a new roof, run new electrical, try to save the floor, and gut and replace the dryboard with drywall. I saw lots of scraping, sanding, staining, and shellacking in my near future. I often found myself peering into the hardware store window at daybreak, quadruple espresso in one hand, empty bucket in the other, waiting to replenish my supply of window glazing. Was it labor of love, or love of labor?

Actually, we found "the resurrection" to be a much needed escape from our busy jobs in advertising, with the added bonus of feeling like we were saving a little piece of my hometown. Throughout the rehab, I continually went back to the planning board. Tackle a chunk, plan the next one. So after replacing the half-sawn log siding on the exterior, I moved on to narrowing down the finishes I wanted for the end product making endless lists of to-dos along the way.

TRA THROW
COLOR

- BED
- TABLE (END)
- DRESSER
- CHAIR
- STOOLS (CAMPING)

tans,
browns,
grays

EXTERIOR ACCENT:
HUNTER GREEN

Floor
stain

SISAL
RUG

A   B   C   D

HUNT
SILHOUETTE WINDOW
SHADINGS

WRITING DESK, SIDE TABLE
(MISSION STYLES)

IMAGINING THE INTERIOR

In reality, our planning process was anything but planned. It was more of a scrap-tearing, sample-hoarding, sketch-on-napkin-making process of estimating what we needed to do. Remember that scene in *A Beautiful Mind* when Russell Crowe tore out all those magazine scraps and wallpapered himself into the little garage room? Then he drew. And wrote. And sketched. And obsessed. Some call it insane. Some call it inspiration. I think it's both. My friend William calls it "crazyface collaging."

> *My friend William calls it "crazyface collaging."*

It's the process of forecasting the color of the trim, the floor stain, the light fixture selection—the endless decisions that have to be made before one should actually pick up a hammer. It's actually a fun, even theraputic approach to planning. So I filled many a cocktail napkin, notebook, and photo album with crazy—then picked up the hammer again.

LEFT: *Elements that would inform our room design.*

BELOW: *Samples of woods and rug materials that inspired the interior palette.*

53

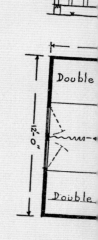

SCRAPING, SCRAPING, AND MORE SCRAPING

We were eager to paint the house. But as anyone who has done any home renovations knows, there's a lot of work to do before you paint. So we scraped the old paint off inside and out, patched the damaged areas with wood putty filler, and replaced entire rotten sections of wood. Then we pressure washed all the exterior wood to strip off any loose paint chips before priming. The first coat of paint proved to be a mini-facelift, which we found encouraging. For the first time we could see the color coming back into our little cabin's face.

Was all this work tedious? You bet. Was it worth it in the long run? Absolutely.

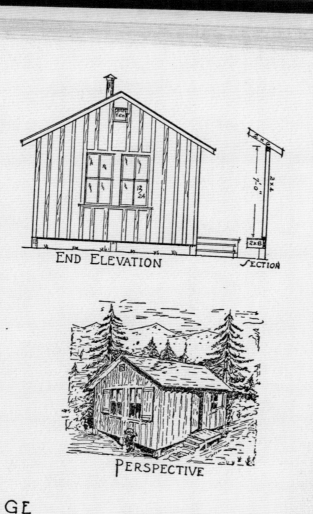

ELEVATION

END ELEVATION

SECTION

Sheathing
Floor

12
24

13
24

2×4

7'-0"

2×4

2×8

Sink

Cupboard

Stove

Storage
over

Cl.

RCH

AN

PERSPECTIVE

SLALOM LODGE

Scale ¼"=1'-0"

OPPOSITE AND ABOVE:

We became window-hanging, paint-scraping, hardware-installing, drywalling machines.

55

LEFT: *Another lovely example of typical log cabin construction from a vintage trade periodical.*

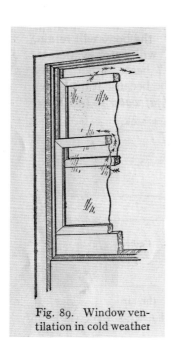

Fig. 89. Window ventilation in cold weather

ABOVE: *Diagram of window ventilation in cold weather. This is where knowledge of mullions and muntins comes in handy.*

WHAT'S THE DIFFERENCE BETWEEN A MUNTIN AND A MULLION? AND WHY SHOULD YOU CARE?

Muntins vs Mullions: In the course of this little adventure, I've learned lots of things about life, love, perserverence—and, more importantly, the difference between muntins and mullions. In case you also lack knowledge in this area, *muntins* are the strips of wood that separate and hold panels of glass in a divided window. *Mullions* are the structural elements that divide adjacent window units. Now you know. Should you ever need to replace one, bring a sample to the lumberyard. If you're lucky (like us), they'll have a match in stock, or will be able to order one from a supplier. Worst case? Send out for a custom router bit so you can make your own.

Hardware: If you still have the original hinges and latches, why not use them? I subscribe to the theory that a little rust and peeling paint adds character. But if you find yourself missing a few pieces (like we did), visit your local architectural salvage shop. Chances are it'll have something that works for you. Another option is big, brand name companies that specialize in manufacturing new vintage-style hardware. As tempting as their glossy catalog pages and gorgeous stores may be, expect to pay five times as much for a similiar piece you could find at your local DIY store.

LEFT: *The joys of saving windows: scraping, painting, installing hardware, and finally, hanging the vintage curtains.*

Rotten Sills: Not pretty. Neglected windowsills are a prime target for rot. As the paint cracks, standing water gets into the wood, and the cycle of freezing, thawing, raining, and drying begins to take its toll. Our sills were partially gone, and the rest pretty far gone. First we scraped away the loose paint with wire brushes and scrapers, and then I mastered my putty knife skills to fill in all of the cracks with marine-grade wood putty. After it dried, we sanded and painted.

The Art of Glazing: This is another seemingly simple task that requires only a little money, but a lot of patience and an equal part of practice. If you don't have a glazing knife, glazing points, and window glazing putty, they can all be had for less than twenty bucks at your local hardware store. And the instructions on the packaging will be better than anything I can tell you here. Be sure to follow the manufacturer's advice with regard to how long you need to wait before painting the putty. I learned this the hard way. Always better to read twice, putty once.

WHAT COLOR IS HOPE?

GRAY   GREEN   YELLOW   BROWN   FOREST   TAN   BLUE

In our case, green. We just needed a little help finding the right shade. We all have a best friend. The one you lean on for advice, who points you in the right direction when you just can't make up your own mind. Mine comes in the form of a 2" x 2" x 6" book of color chips that I keep on me at all times. It is my trusty Pantone book. My little friend helps me identify textile shades, steal that perfect hue of sienna off the Starbucks bathroom wall, and knock off the latest Ralph Lauren fall paint collection (oh, wait, I would never do that). First, I match the chip to the color I find, then take the chip to my local DIY warehouse where I match it to the vendor paint swatches. In the cabin's case, my Pantone book allowed me to match the historically accurate shade of hunter green for the exterior. We had discovered the original color by peeling away four layers of paint to reveal the original shade for the trim underneath.

Some may say you have an unhealthy dependency when the first thing you do when entering a friend's home is whip out the Pantone book and wander down the hallways. (I like to think of it as a compliment to my friend's taste as well as a moment of inspiration). I'm married to my Pantone book. You will be, too, the next time you have the daunting task of choosing which of the 125 different whites is just the right one.

"Man is so made that he can only find relaxation from one kind of labor by taking up another."

ANATOLE FRANCE, POET AND NOVELIST

My husband, David, demonstrates the labor of love, as he paints the half sawn logs (we chose Barn White for those). With the pressure washing, scraping, painting, window repair, roof replacement, and door fixing, it took five long weekends to finish the exterior of the cabin. At 20 hours per weekend, we became familiar with every square inch of the cabin and even more emotionally attached to it.

With the exterior color chosen, it was time to move inside, so it was back to the drawing board again—literally. I sketched the basic layout of the interior before choosing the paint colors. Knowing how it would be furnished helped me settle on the

Draw twice, paint once

color palette. I had already decided on a texture palette of leather, wood, metal, and wool (inspired by the cabin's history as well as its new home). The colors that would best complement these were hunter green, espresso brown, and cream. These also happened to be close to the original colors the cabin would have been in the 1920s. Simple, modest hues that were more functional than cosmetic. Brown baseboards were easy to clean, white and cream were easy to touch up if needed, and green matched everything.

RIGHT: *With only an 11 x 11 foot room to work with, I wanted to get all the details ironed out, including making room for the potbelly stove.*

BELOW: *With five billion shades on the market, after much deliberation and mind changing, here are the three I landed on. A basic white base plus an oaky brown, and what my dad would have called a dark John Deere green.*

FOREST

Turns out the color of hope is green and it looks like this.

FINDING INSPIRATION:

THE COLORS OUTSIDE YOUR WINDOW

If you are overwhelmed by the bazillion options you find in your color swatch book or by swatches you get at the paint store, you can instead find inspiration in a very obvious place—right in front of your nose. Just look out the window and hold those swatches up to the glass. Without fail, I have found that when you take inspiration from the world around you, especially in an outdoor setting, your interior will find harmony with the exterior. This technique helps me decorate for the seasons. Fall = oranges, reds, browns. Winter = white, gray, blue, red. Spring = pink, lavender, white. Summer = yellow, vibrant green, sky blue. Some of these colors are the ones we chose for the cabin.

YELLOW

BLUE

THE JOY OF DRYWALL

You can go pretty easily from old walls, to gutting, to insulating, to roughing in new walls all in a weekend, so you get a great sense of accomplishment in a short amount of time.

Demolition: Tearing out the old walls is fast, easy, and surprisingly theraputic. Tools needed: a hammer, a crowbar, safety goggles, and a bottle of red wine for when it's all over.

Insulation: When the cabin was first built, it wasn't insulated. But with our Wisconsin winters, not insulating was not an option. Just roll it out, press it in the cavities between the studs, and tack it in. We also installed new electrical at this stage.

Drywall: Getting good results with drywall normally requires two things that I lack: patience and more patience. So I'll share a trick when it comes to getting a vintage cabin look with modern drywall: You can forego all the tedious and time consuming taping, mudding and sanding. Instead, plan the location of the seams for a symmetrical look, and nail in one-inch wide wood trim painted the same shade as the surface to cover the seams. You can even align the wall seams with the ceiling seams and use the trim on the ceiling, too. This is a common 1920s cottage technique, so we got an authentic period look as a bonus. The big lesson here: modern drywalling is best left to the pros.

RIGHT: *Tacking in the finishing strips to conceal the drywall seams.*

ELECTRICAL: SOME THINGS ARE BETTER LEFT FOR MY HUSBAND TO DO

As you've probably noticed by now, I'm not opposed to swinging a hammer or digging a ditch. But when it comes to electrical, that's when I let my husband, David, and the World's Most Helpful Neighbor, Joe, take over. I didn't want to be responsible for anything that could potentially burn the cabin down. Luckily, we had nearby electrical for overhead outdoor lighting. So the guys simply extended the wiring to the cabin and wired up two junction boxes and a couple of lights. Since we had gutted the interior walls down to the studs, it was relatively easy for them to run electrical through the walls before we hung the new drywall. Or so they tell me. I won't even attempt to offer electrical how-to advice here, since I don't want to be responsible for burning your house down, either.

LEFT: *My dear husband in his favorite spot—on a ladder fixing things. In this case, he's attaching a powerline through the trees so our little cabin can get light.*

ABOVE: *This is the best neighbor in the world, otherwise known as Joe Koehnke. He is installing a lantern next to the cabin's entrance. Lantern: $15. Having a neighbor like Joe install it for you: priceless.*

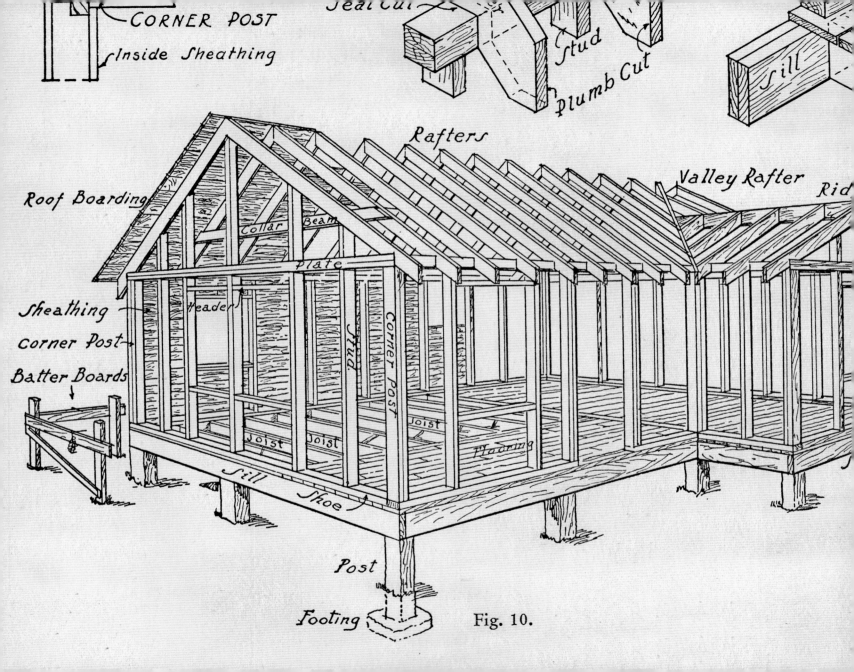

CORNER POST

Inside Sheathing

Seat Cut

Stud

Plumb Cut

Sill

Rafters

Valley Rafter

Rid

Roof Boarding

Collar Beam

plate

Sheathing

Header

Corner Post

corner Post

Stud

Batter Boards

Joist

Joist

Joist

Flooring

Sill

Shoe

Post

Footing

Fig. 10.

FACELIFTS AND NAIL GUNS

It's a small room. How hard could it be to install a roof and replace some siding using a good old-fashioned hammer? Two hours and a pair of very sore paws later, I had given up. I needed some power assist in the form of a nail gun. Seduced by the Sunday shopper ads for "4.9 lbs. with magnesium housing," I'd convinced myself that I needed one. When my husband gave me the choice of either buying a fantastic pair of seventies snakeskin heels or an equally cool (and powerful) nail gun, the

Five things a nail gun can save you: time, backaches, energy, and money—for manicures and for marriage counselors.

moment of truth had arrived. Both were shiny, pretty, and useful. So I did what any practical woman would do—bought both and hid the shoes.

Take note: The first time you use a nail gun, be prepared for kick back—something very similar to being flung backward into a wall. Secure your footing first, lest you find yourself (as I did) with a bruised tailbone from, well…falling on my tail.

ABOVE: *Nails per minute with power nail gun: 30. Nails per minute the old-fashioned way: 5–10 (depending on the swinger).*

OPPOSITE: *Materials and methods common to old cabin construction.*

69

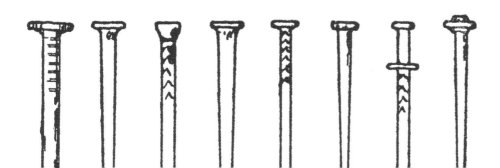

REFINISHING A WOOD FLOOR IS A PAIN

In the back. And in the arms. And…yeah. At first we didn't actually know if the floor was salvageable. It was so beat up, we had prepared ourselves for the reality that we just might have to replace it altogether or use the original as a subfloor, laying new wood flooring on top. But that option just seemed wrong. With the rest of the cabin restored to its original condition, a brand spanking new hardwood floor seemed unfaithful to the notion of "modest." So we decided to embrace the old and refinish it—which would prove to be neither fast or easy.

20 hours, 2 coats of stain, and 3 coats of polyurethane later… we found the floor.

RIGHT: *Our finished floor. Finally.*

FAR LEFT: *I have to admit, the most rewarding moment was when we had done the floor but hadn't yet moved a stick of furniture in. To stand back and look at her "new" again was a dream.*

NEAR LEFT: *Now I can add the glamorous title of floor sander to my resume. But the job still required good old-fashioned hand labor as well, in the form of homemade sanding blocks.*

HOW TO REFINISH A WOOD FLOOR

SAND IT

STEP 1: Pound in all nails and pull out any carpet staples.

STEP 2: Rent a floor sander, unless you have a lot of patience and Popeye arms. Start with the heaviest grit sandpaper (try 36 grit).

STEP 3: Run the sander over the floor in the direction of the wood grain—*not* across the grain. If you gouge while sanding like I did, smooth it out with long strokes.

STEP 4: Switch to a lighter-grit paper (try 60) and give it another pass. To get a really smooth floor, move up the grits sequentially from 36 to 60 to 80 to 100.

STEP 5: Repeat steps 3 and 4 with an edging machine if your floor sander doesn't reach the edge of the floor.

STAIN IT

STEP 6: Brush, sweep, vaccum, and then wipe down the whole floor with a tack rag to pick up the dust. Cleaner floor = better finish, trust me.

STEP 7: Open all the windows so you don't asphyxiate yourself. Do a test application in a corner and wait 5 minutes to make sure you like it before you proceed with the whole shebang.

STEP 8: Apply your first coat. Use a brush if you want to apply darker coats (smooth out with a rag). Or use a rag if you want more control. Apply with long, even strokes, going with the grain.

STEP 9: After the first coat dries, decide if you want a second, and touch up lighter areas you may have missed.

FINISH IT

STEP 10: Make sure the floor is *completely* dry. Shake the polyurethane can. Keep shaking. Shake more.

STEP 11: Apply polyurethane with a brush or roller, using smooth, even strokes with the grain to avoid marks in the finish.

STEP 12: Allow the finish to dry (usually about 3 hours) before putting on a second coat. Let it dry overnight before walking on it, and for three days before dragging your furniture in.

HOW TO SAVE A GERIATRIC COTTAGE DOOR

(In 12 Not-So-Easy Steps)

1. Clean*
2. Disassemble
3. Strip
4. Scrape
5. Sand
6. Prime
7. Paint
8. Clean
9. Paint
10. Reassemble
11. Hang on hinges
12. Post vacancy sign and enjoy

*I find a little beer makes this step go faster.

LEFT: *The sorry state of the door before rehab, and David at work on all the tedious scraping. At center is the finished door at last—well, except for one of the muntins.*

TOOLBOX ESSENTIALS

hinge   scraper   sandpaper

stripper   foam brush   paint

nails   beer   sanding block

hammer   paintbrush

scrub brush   screwdriver

GETTING A FAT POTBELLY THRU

A SKINNY DOOR

When we moved the cabin, it had a neat little vintage gas stove, circa 1945. It was rusty, banged up, and abused. We thought about restoring it, for about five minutes, then trashed it. Fortunately, my husband David, in his infinite wisdom, had purchased a potbelly stove back in 1999 to prepare for a potential Y2K disaster—which, of course, never occurred. (I think David was disappointed, as he was hoping to try his survivalist skills.) But he was happy to move the potbelly from our Chicago home and haul it up to Wisconsin. It was the first piece of "furniture" in the cabin.

Stovepipe Common Sense:

- *The "male" or crimped end of the stovepipe should always point toward the stove to keep creosote running inside the pipe rather than leaking out. (Creosote is the black gunk that builds up when you burn stuff.)*

- *Stovepipes get hot so keep black pipe at least 18 inches from combustibles.*

- *Did I mention stovepipes get hot? They can be installed only where they're visible—not inside a closet or attic, or as a wall pass-through. We had to use a special double-wall insulated pipe section to run it through the ceiling and out the roof.*

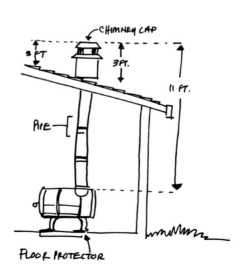

THE POTBELLY STOVE

Because of its characteristic shape, the stove became known as the potbelly. With a round oven in the center of the body, it can burn either wood or coal and can even be converted to gas (very fuel efficient). They come in three sizes, with burn times ranging from 6 to 8 hours for the small and up to 14 hours for the largest potbelly stoves. They were originally used to heat railroad stations and general stores and became central to gathering places like schools, churches, workshops, and barns. Made of solid cast iron like most of this size, ours weighs about 250 pounds.

Chapter Four

DIGGING FOR TREASURE

WITH A

VINTAGE TROWEL

I did my homework, researching how a typical tourist camp proprietor would have furnished the little cabin. Then I set out shopping.

THE FUN PART: SHOPPING

All my digging pointed to the same few things: a wrought iron bed, a desk (so plain it could have been disposable), a chair, a dresser and maybe a side table. Not that there's room in the cabin for more. Armed with my shopping list, my drawings and a whole lot of hope, I emptied the Wagoneer and headed out on one of the best kinds of scavenger hunts ever. (Although my husband might argue that this kind of shopping is merely a form of self-inflicted pain.)

OPPOSITE: *I started where I always do: with a before photograph. Add a little over-confidence, mix in the magic of Photoshop, and voilà! I knew where the pictures would hang long before I'd lifted a crowbar to gut the moldy dryboard.*

LEFT: *A vintage outdoor catalog made a wish book for the project. I was able to find the picnic baskets, thermoses, and lanterns pictured here.*

PREVIOUS PAGE: *When your travels yield more treasures that you can fit in your luggage, pick up vintage suitcases like the leather case I found in a Czech antique shop. Extra baggage is cheaper to ship than crates.*

Our Wagoneer's leaf springs would become the sacrificial lamb to the weight of my bargains.

I had years of training for this challenge, having mastered the art of flea market haggling around the globe: remote countrysides in France and Holland, fishing villages on the southern coast of Ireland, scary parking lots on the outskirts of Prague, the gypsy-laden old town square in Buenos Aires, local rural markets in Mexico, tourist-traps in Madrid, handicrafts markets in Florence, and even cheesy tour bus stops in Athens and Hong Kong.

MARKET OF THE FLEA VARIETY

How to outfit a cabin for under $300: yard sales, charity resale shops, church fund-raiser tag sales, junk stores, thrift stores...and yes, even dumpster diving. But none compare to the holy grail of all things cheap and cool—the flea market. So off I went to the almighty Walworth County Flea Market in Wisconsin. My self-imposed rule? Any purchase had to be authentic to the era of the cabin, or it wouldn't cross the threshold. At least that was the rationale I gave my husband, who couldn't understand why we didn't just go to IKEA and get it over with. The deal we struck was that I had a $300 budget. If I exceeded it, he would burn the cabin down. (Not really of course, but sometimes he likes to be dramatic when making a point.) I accepted this challenge with utmost enthusiasm.

Whoever chose the name *flea* for those glorious open-air markets must have been high. What exactly is enticing or appealing about fleas? Had the person put in charge of branding this outdoor form of antiquing not considered the obvious *treasure trove* or even *resale haven*? After a bet with my husband, we consulted our best and smartest friend, Google. She led us to Wikipedia: "One popular theory is that the term *flea market* is literally translated from the French *marché aux puces* (an outdoor bazaar in Paris), named after the 'wingless bloodsucker' parasite that infested the upholstery of the ratty old resale furniture." How compelling.

Once the shopping started, I became an obnoxious braggard. "I found this for two dollars!" came out of my mouth more times than I care to admit. Salvation Army shipment day, church charity auctions, garage sales, tag sales, "my neighbor's ninety-eight-year-old great aunt died and we cleared out her basement" sales—you name it, I went. Even the random dumpster on a spring cleanup day could not be passed up.

America has more than five thousand flea, antique, and open-air markets and swap meets. So many markets, so little time.

I was fully, unapologetically addicted. The problem, I suppose, as with most addictions, is that after your first flea market high, your judgment becomes impaired. Soon you might find yourself slamming on your brakes on a three-lane Interstate, darting between cars to retrieve what appears to be (from a hundred yards away) an antique Hudson Bay wool blanket.

RIGHT: *Apple bucket for wood: $5; picnic basket for books: $6; wagon to haul everything around in: priceless.*

BELOW: *My favorite thing: digging through piles of vintage linens at resale shops. This is where I found the bedding for the cabin.*

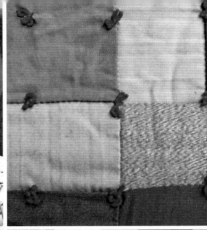

In full flea market mode I purchased the vintage fan for $12, the patchwork quilt for $15, and three food crates for $20. Somehow, time spent shopping passes so much faster than time spent refinishing a floor.

IF YOU HAPPEN TO SUFFER FROM TWO OR MORE OF THESE PHOBIAS, YOU MAY NOT ENJOY FLEA MARKETING:

- *Laliophobia:* fear of talking
- *Mysophobia*: fear of uncleanliness
- *Phenogophobia*: fear of daylight
- *Social phobia*: fear of crowds
- *Retrophobia*: fear of old things

THE FINE ART OF DUMPSTER DIVING
AND HOW TO HAGGLE LIKE A PRO

Believe it or not, there is an art to dumpster diving. Bear in mind, diving doesn't always involve dumpsters: The activity also includes "curb shopping" on spring cleanup day, and moving day on university campuses. The first time you dive, you look sheepishly around to see if anybody is watching. If you have no witnesses, maybe you poke a stick at (what appears to be) a gorgeous, Mission-style oak chair or desk remnant. The next time, maybe you actually send your husband in to retrieve that lovely discarded vintage apple crate. One day (and you can't really pinpoint the moment the addiction takes full control) you find yourself tossing all humility to the wind as you jump headfirst into

no man's land, determined to nab that plaid retro thermos before anybody else gets their paws on it. I mean, it's gotta be worth at least $13 once it's hosed off, right? The rational side of your brain that sets off the "don't" alarm anytime you get near a garbage dumpster in a sketchy neighborhood slows down— and then stops working entirely.

You have to dig deep, sometimes going places you never thought you'd find yourself: the bottom of a sale bin at the Goodwill store, under a tangled pile of old picture frames (which yielded a perfectly beat up little walnut frame for the dresser that set me back all of $3). Of course, under the spell of a buying frenzy

LEFT: *Some of my dumpster finds. We installed the screen door in the cabin and the terracotta planter holds geraniums on the front stoop.*

we sometimes make mistakes. That old-fashioned hunting-themed ashtray, for instance, would keep me awake at night wondering if somebody would actually use it for its intended purpose and set the cabin ablaze. Bed + smoking = bad idea. I threw it out.

Then there will always be that one thing you wanted, stared at, contemplated, walked away from because it was $3 too much, and came back for only to find it being carried off in some other lucky hunter's cart. Those ghosts of treasures unclaimed will haunt you. My advice is that if you see it and you get that familiar tingly feeling of, *Oh, my God! I have to have it*—then just buy it. The exception to this rule is that the item of your desire cannot exceed your own personal dollar threshold of pain—for me, the $25 mark. If the price is higher than your limit, then you risk feeling all the guilt associated with buyer's remorse. Good rule of thumb: The less you spend, the less you care if you change your mind once the blessed buy gets home.

Another helpful hint: Carrying a $5 cup of Starbucks coffee is not helpful when you're trying to negotiate a discounted price. You will get the best deals when dressed more like a vagabond than a yuppie. Be willing to get your hands dirty. Flea markets are not known for cleanliness, so the less of a prima donna you are, the more likely you will get the sympathy discount. Work it—it's worth it.

RIGHT: *Some of the treasures for the cabin and what I got them for.*

BOOKS: (top left)
original price: $4 each
haggled price: 3 for $10

PAINT BY NUMBER (bottom left)
original price: $20
haggled price: $15

BISCUIT BOX (center)
original price: $25
haggled price: $19

BOY SCOUT CANTEEN
(bottom center) original price: $8
haggled price: $5

VINTAGE FISHING REEL
(bottom right) original price: $15
haggled price: $11

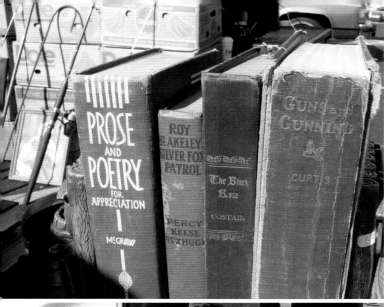

PROSE AND POETRY FOR APPRECIATION
McGRAW

ROY BLAKELEY SILVER FOX PATROL
PERCY KEESE FITZHUGH

The Black Rose
COSTAIN

GUNS and GUNNING
CURTIS

COTTER
MILWAUKEE
FINE BISCUIT

TEL. 6062922251
ANTIK PLAC

OFFICIAL TRAIL CANTEEN

$8.00

Genuine Jik CASTING

THE JOYS OF BARKCLOTH
AND OTHER SURPRISING THINGS I HAVE
IN COMMON WITH GRANDMA

Is it weird that one can get such a thrill from finding a piece of discarded barkcloth in an old attic? It all started with a small roll of fabric I found up there. I didn't know it at the time, but that former table runner would be resurrected into curtains, a bed pillow, a drawer liner and yes, even a coin purse liner. I soon found myself researching period textiles and palettes and shopping for them at antique stores and flea markets.

As it turned out, our forest-themed barkcloth is a rarity. Barkcloth is a soft, thick, densely woven fabric having a rough texture like that of tree bark (hence the name). Vintage barkcloth is usually found in the form of drapery. If you find it being sold by the yard, it is most likely a new fabric known as NOS (New Old Stock). How do you tell the difference between original and NOS? Who cares? If it works for you, it works, plus the newer fabrics will last longer. Because it's so pricey, check your dimensions to get the minimum necessary for your project. If you need only a yard or two for a pillow cover or table runner, check for "cutters" first. These are typically scraps with holes in them that you can work around. Also check for dry rot and fading. A little fading can add up to a much better deal. Avoid the pieces with dry rot.

ABOVE: *I found this vintage barckcloth in the attic and worked it into the cabin decor.*

OPPOSITE: *Barkcloth comes in countless styles.*

93

All those long weekends of haggling my way through flea markets all over the state had finally come to fruition in this one little room. In the end, my favorite find was the vintage bedspread that perfectly matched the antique barkcloth colors. My husband cannot understand how one could get so excited about glass knobs, but it was like Christmas day when I found the six little green jewels for the the dresser at a yard sale for $5.

THE FINISHED ROOM

No kitchen, no bathroom, no TV. Just a single bedroom with a desk, chair, dresser, potbelly stove, and an abundance of character.

TOP ROW: *Vintage books scored at thrift store for $1 each, my grandmother's antique secretary desk, and a potbelly stove.*

BOTTOM ROW: *A $15 junk store antique mirror, a $12 paint-by-number found on eBay, and a retro fan (new fan, old style).*

ADD: GREEN SHUTTERS
+ FLOWER BOX

WALKING
PATH:
STONE
PAVE

Chapter Five

PLANTING THE SEED

With the cabin rehabbed inside and out, it was time to get her dressed. I dreamed of a skirt of bright green hostas and a stone path around her. I would find out the hard way that a stone path is easier drawn than built.

"Opportunity is missed by most people because it is dressed in overalls and looks like work."

THOMAS A. EDISON, INVENTOR

MY THUMB IS NOT EVEN CHARTREUSE

If given the choice to garden or chew glass, I would prefer the latter. When faced with the challenge of how to convert a weed field into a semblance of a landscaped plot, I did what any self-respecting nongardener would do: I traded cocktails for labor. Fortunately, my lack of desire to garden is compensated for by the willingness of our friends and family to pitch in.

Because I was nearly paralyzed with the daunting task of "the G word," I started where I always do—with sketches. But this time, I just drew them over the top of some photos of the cabin (as on page 96). It helped me visualize ideas in scale and figure out where I might park a picnic table, Adirondack chairs, and the oh-so-necessary hammock. I'd heard rumors that hosta plants thrive on neglect—perfect for my gardening skill level. Daylilies also turned out to be the perfect gardening crutch, since they are virtually impossible to kill and come back every year for more abuse.

OPPOSITE AND LEFT:

The first real work was to clear the weed field so we could bring in topsoil to spread as a foundation for the grass seed. No small task, I assure you. Our friend Heather gets her hands dirty planting hostas.

BELOW: *I sketched an overhead thumbnail of the landscape design before we started, which helped me wrap my head around the task ahead.*

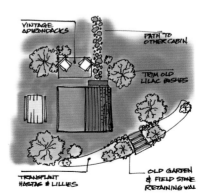

VINTAGE ADIRONDACKS

PATH TO OTHER CABIN

TRIM OLD LILAC BUSHES

TRANSPLANT HOSTAS & LILLIES

OLD GARDEN & FIELD STONE RETAINING WALL

TREES: OAK, MAPLE, COTTONWOOD, BIRCH

THE TREEMEN COMETH

The cabin's lake view was totally obstructed by overgrowth. Whom do you call when you've got dead branches hovering precariously over your cabin's head? It turns out,

Before we could start landscaping, we had a few tree challenges to address.

you call the treemen (or if you're lucky they just show up on your doorstep, like my little brother Sam, who is, thankfully, a pro). As if uprooting and relocating the cabin to it's northern perch wasn't enough, Sam arrived with three other professional treemen to swing from the tree branches like fearless squirrels, chainsaws dangling from their belts. Within an hour of their arrival, the cabin was open to a fresh, unobstructed view of the lake.

ABOVE AND LEFT:

Checklists to track my tasks make me happy, productive, and über-organized. I soon learned that I would need a lot more than these clippers.

RIGHT: *A much needed haircut for the trees surrounding the cottage: the four treemen to the rescue! (No treemen were harmed when taking this photo.) From left: Sam, Darin, Dave, and Mike.*

We thought the Rock Farmer was the stuff of legend. I mean, how exactly does one farm rocks?

THE ROCK FARMER OF WALWORTH COUNTY

One building material that we needed right away was rocks—for the cabin's foundation, firepit, and back steps, and to contain the rings of hostas that we were planning to plant around the trees. Seemed easy enough. Wisconsin is full of rocks, right? Well, yes, if you don't mind paying $9 apiece at the local DIY lumberyard. Another option was stealing from the neighbors. (Not really an option of course, but I have to admit that it crossed my mind while I was rock hunting in my own backyard and digging them individually from the ground). But then we began to hear rumors of a man they called the Rock Farmer. At first we wrote him off as legend. I mean, how exactly does one farm rocks? Having no luck finding what we needed elsewhere, we decided to hitch the trailer to the pickup and go find this guy. As it turns out, he did exist, between Fontana and Elkhorn, Wisconsin, on a back road that you can find only if you stop and ask about a dozen people along the way: "Take a left at the melon stand, a right at Pearce's silos, he's next to the old dairy farm." I might as well have been given directions to Texas via farm roads. But when we rounded the bend, we did in fact find a glorious mound of rocks of all shapes and sizes. After dragging our trailer down every God-forsaken farm road in Walworth County, finding this mythical rock farm was like finding Santa Claus. Only the Rock Farmer was nowhere to be found.

Rocks to build the patio firepit…

for the cabin foundation…

103

the terraced steps…

and ringing hosta beds and trees.

This is how it played out on our first visit: scour the farm looking for the farmer, run from the dog who clearly wanted to eat my thigh, wait, sit in the car and honk, wait again, call the phone number, wait, eventually give up and guess what the rocks cost, stuff some cash and a note in an envelope for the rocks we were about to take without permission, and sprint to the mailbox (avoiding the dog) to deposit a note with our confession. We would repeat this weekly pilgrimage to the ghost Rock Farmer for a month until we finally had enough—of slinging rocks chain-gang style, and the rocks themselves. (Some of them weighed 40 pounds.) I did finally meet him. A charming man. A man of very few words. Actually, only one: "Thanks."

It's surprising how so many rocks don't spread very far. We had to go back many times to get enough for the cabin's various projects.

ENTER HOSTA MAN

Next, our cabin needed to get dressed for the season—a flirty skirt of hostas in shades of green and yellow was what I had in mind. We'd read about yet another guy—the Plant Whisperer—who supposedly cultivated miles of rolling hostas in every variation known to man. We'd also heard this hosta heaven was hidden behind an autobody shop in the middle of nowhere. So we set out in much the same way we had with the Rock Farmer, on a winding path of wrong turns. Three stops for directions and two mistaken addresses later, we found him. Al is the proprietor of a fine autobody shop, which is his main occupation, and in his off-hours, he is a plant doctor of sorts. He asked a series of questions about our cabin site: where it was, how close it was to the water, which direction it faced, what the soil was like, and so on.

This interview felt like a secret initiation at which we had to answer a dozen questions correctly or would be denied the privilege of access. After a complete diagnosis, he prescribed a few variations of hostas and led us on a little path back behind rusted vehicles, greenhouses, and heaps of wagons. We rounded the bend to find a most unexpected site: acres of rolling, manicured hostas in elaborate planting beds that would make the Chicago Botanical Gardens fire their staff and start over. "So, you wet sand fiberglass panels for 12 hours a day and, um, in your off-hours have found the time to cultivate over four hundred varieties of hostas and build a world-class arboretum in your backyard?" I asked him. "That's about right, I guess," Al replied. I instantly loved this man.

ABOVE: *Hostas border the path to the cabin.*

OPPOSITE: *This is what heaven for gardeners must look like. Al's backyard is a haven for all things hosta.*

NUMBER OF YEARS ONE SHOULD WAIT BEFORE DIVIDING HOSTA: 3

NUMBER OF HOSTAS PURCHASED: 30

NUMBER AL CHARGED ME FOR: 5

NUMBER OF VISITORS AL GETS IN A YEAR: 545

RECORD IN A SINGLE DAY: 250

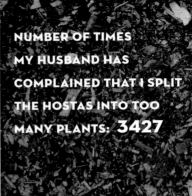

NUMBER OF TIMES MY HUSBAND HAS COMPLAINED THAT I SPLIT THE HOSTAS INTO TOO MANY PLANTS: 3427

Made in the shade

BOB SOLBERG, OF GREEN HILL HOSTAS IN CHAPEL HILL, N.C., OPENS OUR EYES TO A HOST OF HOSTAS THAT DON'T NEED MUCH SUN TO SHINE

COUNTRY MOUSE
A mini with heart-shaped leaves, grows to 8 inches wide. Perfect for small containers.

NUMBER OF MEMBERS IN THE AMERICAN HOSTA SOCIETY IN 1968: 4

NUMBER OF MEMBERS TODAY: 3,000

NUMBER OF VARIETIES AL CULTIVATES: 400

HEIGHT IN INCHES OF THE 'ALLIGATOR SHOES' HOSTA SPECIES: 18

NUMBER OF HOSTAS NAMED 'ELVIS LIVES': 1

NUMBER OF MINUTES SPENT PLANTING EACH HOSTA: **10**

NUMBER OF ISSUES OF *THE HOSTA JOURNAL* PUBLISHED EACH YEAR: **3**

NUMBER OF YEARS AL'S SON HAS BEEN HELPING DAD: **5**

AVERAGE COST IN DOLLARS FOR A ONE-GALLON PLANT: **10**

NUMBER OF FRIENDS THAT HELPED PLANT OUR HOSTAS: **6**

BOTTLES OF BEER CONSUMED: **40**

AVERAGE NUMBER OF HOURS PER WEEK A TYPICAL MIDWESTERN GARDENER SPENDS TENDING: **5**

NUMBER OF HOURS PER WEEK AL SPENDS TENDING TO HIS HOSTA EMPIRE: **60**

THE SECRET TO A HEALTHY, HARDY HOSTA SKIRT: BUNNY POOP

Below is a conversation I had with our neighbor, Judy (the Queen of Bunnies), who has an impressive hosta garden and is an expert on how to coax them into growing.

"In some parts, people use chicken poop or cow manure to fertilize their hosta beds. But that kind is called warm manure. You have to let it sit for a year before you can use it. But with my bunny poop, you can use it right away. I have a lot of varieties. People love this stuff so much, they come with their pickup trucks. I've been doing this since my son, Don, was nine, and in the 4-H Club.

He wanted sheep. I said no way, you can have rabbits. Right now I have more rabbits than I care to mention. I guess that's what happens. I raise them, show them, breed them, and give them to 4-H kids. Then, well…let's just say that you can tell early on which ones will be good to show and which will make good stew. I have lots of stew. Would you like some?" (She kindly offered this as I stroked the cutest bunny ever.)

A well-fed hosta is a happy hosta. After a good dose of Judy's magic fertilizing bunny manure, our cabin's landscaped skirt of hostas grew tall…and fast.

ABOVE: *Our friend Will preps a plant, while William uses the longest possible tool to feed the hostas their dose of bunny manure.*

LEFT: *Judy's bunny ribbons, one of her babies in its cage, trophies, cages, and tools of the bunny-poop trade.*

The vote for a fire pit and patio would win over the wrap-around pathway (too expensive, too time-consuming). But in the end, the path was not missed.

Chapter Six

365 DAYS OF LIFE

AT THE CABIN

One of the best reasons for the cabin is that it brings people together, around the lake and around the campfire. With each season comes new opportunities to escape from city life, explore nature, and entertain friends and family.

"And so seasons went rolling on into summer, as one rambles into higher and higher grass."

HENRY DAVID THOREAU, AUTHOR, POET, PHILOSOPHER

CANNONBALLS, SANDY TOES, AND POISON IVY

Who needs air conditioning when you have a breeze that smells of fresh pine and lakeside flowers? Summertime is when we use the cabin most often, and we go there every chance we get. A typical summer day on the lake: Wake up to birdsong. Make some coffee. Head down to the lake. Mostly, we spend our time outside, using the cabin just as a room to lay our heads at the end of a long day of swimming, boating, fishing, grilling out, and being completely and unapologetically lazy. In the land of Lake Wandawega cabin life, cellphones are banished, conference calls are forbidden, and the beer is always cold. What we allow: cannonballs off the pier, sandy toes, and picking daisies.

We do have to keep alert for our nemesis, poison ivy, but I don't want to tarnish the idyllic image, so I won't go into the details about two long days spent reading the Boy Scouts' first aid manual and soaking neck high in calamine lotion.

OPPOSITE: *The cabin is primarily used as a guesthouse. Here it is ready for a summer picnic.*

BELOW: *Signs of summer… you'll always find croquet balls and life jackets littering the grounds like leaves.*

The best of summer: flip flops, rowboats, archery, tennis, firecrackers. If ever you want to relive the best of your childhood, find yourself a little cabin and soak up the season. All of these scenes you see here were captured in and around our little cabin.

CIDER, JACK-O'-LANTERNS, AND ANGRY SQUIRRELS

It wasn't until the cabin was wearing its seasonal coat of orange and yellow maple leaves that I realized I had subconsciously dressed her in a fall wardrobe. Every stick of furniture, curtain, pillow, and book was of the autumn color palette. She blended in perfectly.

With the cabin finished and our first summer behind us, we realized we had even more reasons to entertain our friends. After all, it is the season of raking and burning leaves, bonfires and pumpkins. We discovered that as fast as we carved pumpkins for jack-o'-lanterns, the squirrels would eat their triangle-eyed faces off to fatten themselves up for the frigid months ahead. They clearly had no appreciation for the time it took us to carve them. I swear that some would stare right at me with malice in their eyes as they chewed their way through my smiley-faced gourds. As the days grew shorter, we stayed up later, sitting in the Adirondack chairs that flank the stone-lined fire pit in front of the cabin. We found the saying about making the most out of something was right on. Truth is, in the end, the transport and renovation of the cabin wasn't really about the cabin itself as much as it was about creating a place to spend time with family and friends—the best reason for any endeavor.

"Everyone must take time to sit and watch the leaves turn." ELIZABETH LAWRENCE, GARDEN DESIGNER AND WRITER

Hay rack rides = fall. Something about this place makes you want to engage in all things fall: leaf raking, wood chopping, hot cider drinking, scarecrow making. Sometimes this includes a visit from a neighbor's pet raccoon. (One friend called it a mauling; we liked to think of it as more of an excited hug.)

123

THE BIG REWARD FOR THIS REHAB JOURNEY: THROWING A PARTY, CABIN STYLE.

The annual fall party is part of what makes the whole adventure of the cabin's move and restoration worth it. Sugar Creek, where the cabin site is, is surrounded by apple orchards, pumpkin patches, maple syrup farms—even a couple of boutique wineries. I am always looking for a reason to visit them all, so party prepping becomes the best excuse to go shopping. After all, there is a lot to do: build the bonfire, make the scarecrow, carve the pumpkins, whittle some marshmallow sticks for the s'mores, visit all the bakeries to get the best local pies. For even more fun, we love to put together a warming beverage bar with hot toddies, spiked cider, and hot chocolate. Our friends like to come early to help with preparation and get in a little fishing. So the party ends up being a weekend-long event.

125

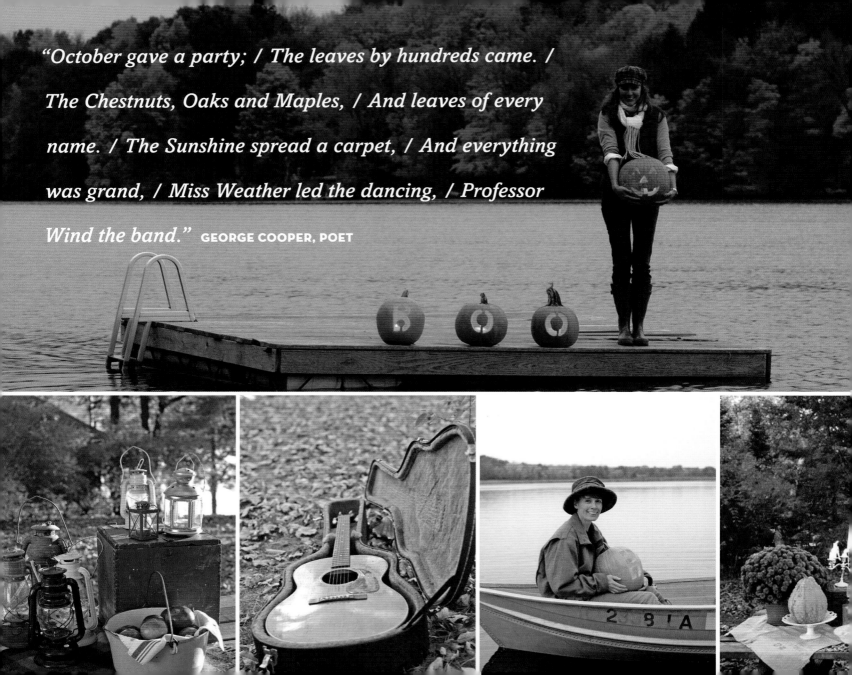

"*October gave a party; / The leaves by hundreds came. / The Chestnuts, Oaks and Maples, / And leaves of every name. / The Sunshine spread a carpet, / And everything was grand, / Miss Weather led the dancing, / Professor Wind the band.*" **GEORGE COOPER, POET**

LEFT: *The author on the diving platform on Lake Wandawega .*

BELOW, CENTER: *Our friend Alison carts our carved masterpeices over to the floating lake raft.*

RIGHT: *David places the final pumpkin on the pier just before our annual fall cabin party. We spend the whole day fishing, playing, and boating, then feast at night.*

After an afternoon hike admiring the Midwest fall colors, nothing says welcome back like a spread of homemade sweets and locally brewed beer. Handy skills include s'more assemby and roasting, and pumpkin carving.

RECIPE FOR A PERFECT FALL PARTY

Mix in one large Wisconsin retreat, a handful of friends, a crisp fall weekend, a dash of bonfire, and a touch of s'mores — stir well.

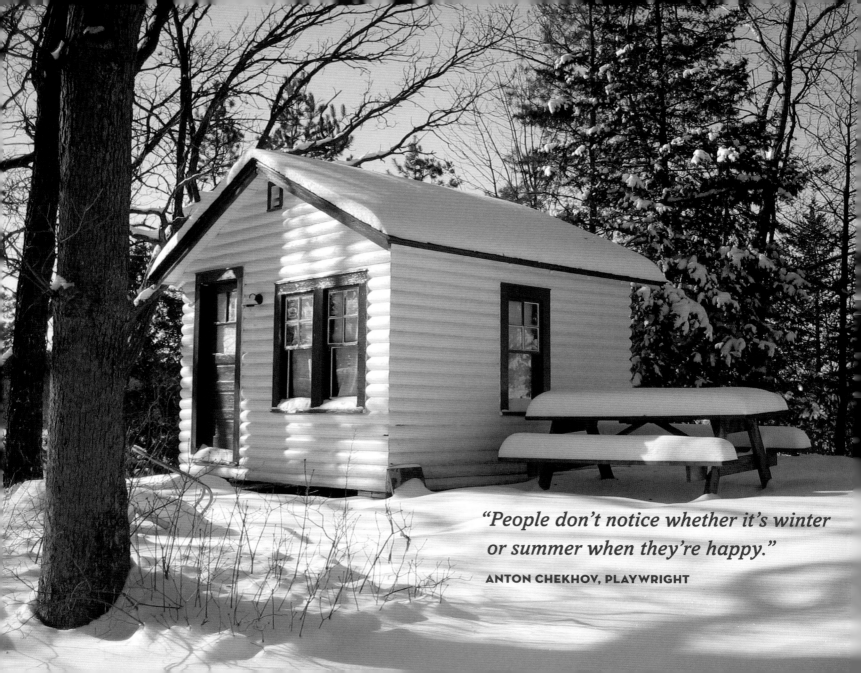

"*People don't notice whether it's winter or summer when they're happy.*"

ANTON CHEKHOV, PLAYWRIGHT

HOT CHOCOLATE, TOBOGGANS, AND CHIPMUNK SQUATTERS

Before we knew it, winter was upon us. We thought we'd shutter up the cabin to weather the season. But when it came time to strip the linens and box up the contents, I just couldn't do it. It felt like visiting a grandmother for a summer and leaving her all alone until next year. So we didn't. What happened next surprised us. The little cabin helped us discover an entirely new season. As we live in Chicago, we typically try to avoid all snow, slush, and ice beyond what we already have to endure—at all costs. But it's amazing how one little wood stove can crank out the heat in a small space. The white landscape offered up a whole different experience. We found ourselves actually wanting to try new sports like snowshoeing, ice-skating, and cross-country skiing. To skate on our pond, we take the four-wheel drive with the plow attachment to smooth out the surface. (I have a collection of vintage ice skates that we all wear.) It's amazing how much you can enjoy something new if you put yourself in an environment with so few options. Sunsets became a substitute for cable TV. Texting yielded to actual conversations. Store-bought double-shot skim lattes were replaced by hot chocolate cooked up on the little stove. In my attempts to re-create an idyllic winter of the past, my husband found himself more than once being coaxed into wearing big fat vintage hand-knit sweaters. Once he found that resistance was futile, they ended up being his favorites.

ABOVE: *I had to have this little bird cabin. It hangs from a branch near the entrance.*

LEFT: *Nothing is more romantic than the first snow of the season draping a blanket over the roof. Well, a furnace might be more romantic, actually.*

131

The cabin is the perfect homebase for doing all things winter. Pictured here are a few of our favorite winter pastimes when hosting guests during the snowy months. Nothing beats spending the day outside, then returning to the cabin to stoke the potbelly stove, curl up with the dog, a book, and some hot chocolate.

DEWDROPS, DAFFODILS, AND PROMISCUOUS TOADS

ABOVE: *Every year without fail so far, the tree swing emerges from a blanket of snow, intact for another season of near-constant action.*

RIGHT: *Also in near-constant action: springtime woodland frogs.*

LEFT: *When we bought the property, we were so very lucky to have inherited dozens of hydrangeas, which burst into bloom in late spring and stay with us all summer long.*

With the snow melting, we witnessed the unveiling of the cabin all over again. As the icicles fell we got to see how she weathered the long Wisconsin winter months. We didn't expect her to hold up entirely, as she was technically geriatric at eighty-five years, but we were pleasantly surprised. Paint didn't chip off. Roofing shingles stayed put. And no critters had burrowed through the floorboard to hole up for the winter with us. The months of April and May were like waking up in the morning—a bit creaky, but wide-eyed soon enough in the clear, fresh air. And there were other really big questions still to be answered. Will my bulbs come up?

Will my daylilies come back after the tremendous beating they took during the construction? Will those hideous lake toads mate like bunnies, hatch, and surround us again? Yes, yes, and yes. And then the cabin's pretty green and white skirt of hostas sprouted up, seemingly overnight. It didn't take us long to get things ready again for more guests. Hang the hammock. Replenish the log stack for the fire pit. Get a good spring cleaning in. Open all the windows and let the fresh air and a new season in (but not all of those new toads).

135

When spring comes, we love to sprawl out in the sun for lunch, which entails dragging an old farm table out to the grass and spending the day doing pretty much nothing. Perfect.

Log Cabin Tourist Camp.
½ Mile East of Bluff Spring's
Route 67

Chapter Seven

FOUR WALLS,
ONE HUNDRED STORIES

With our little adopted cabin now complete and filled with life nearly every weekend, I couldn't help but wonder about its past. If the walls could talk, what stories would they tell? So off I set on a journey to learn more about the cabin's history. It took me nearly as long to do the research as it did to rehab the cabin itself. Ultimately, we discovered that we didn't give the cabin a second life: it was actually its fifth.

A LITLE CABIN THAT COULD: THE MANY LIVES OF OUR VERY MODEST COTTAGE

1

1920s

Beardstown is bustling. Lodging was needed. A tourist cabin was born. Here she is pictured brand-spanking new along with her sister.

1922 & 1926

Then came the floods; they actually brought more business to the tourist cabin camp, which sat on the outskirts of town. Here we see a few waist-deep locals.

2

1930s

The "hot pillow trade" keeps the cabin booked. According to local legend, the pretty things pictured here were parading their wares.

3

1940s

In the decade of duck hunting and gambling, the cabin became a Friday night rod-and-gun club venue for card games.

4

1950s

A start-up trucking company needs an office. Pictured here: A.C. Jones with his grandpa. A.C. later took over the business. The cabin is in the background.

5

1960s

A new office is built, and the cabin becomes a storage shed and is later abandoned.

2006

After three decades of decay, we adopt and rescue the little cabin.

2006

On the road to its new home on Lake Wandawega in Elkhorn, Wisconsin.

2006

Ready, set...home!

2007

A new address on a lake, open again for guests eighty-five years later.

O'Brien J Joseph (Bridget A), wks CB&Q, r 1310 Lafayette
O'Brien Wm,, r 1310 Lafayette
O'Donnell Richard (Rosa), condr CB&Q, r 1100 Wash
Oetgen Augusta C Mrs, r 305 W 5th
Oetgen Rosa Miss, tchr Central School, r 410 Lafayette
Oetgen Sophia (wid John), r 410 Lafayette
Oetgen Catharine, tel opr, r 802 W 2d
Oetgen Raymond CB&Q, r Goodell Hotel

CLUES IN THE RAFTERS LEAD TO...

A TOWN UNDERWATER?

It all started with a simple piece of wood we found while gutting the cabin, a section of drop siding stamped "W. E. Terry Lbr Co. Beardstown, IL." Our search for the cabin's history was on. We began by locating phone books from the 1920s, which revealed the advertisement pictured at left along with an address, which in turn helped us locate a vintage photograph. The fascinating part was uncovering the fate of the lumberyard: It flooded along with the entire town right around the time the cabin was built. If it weren't for the flood of 1922, we wouldn't have found this photograph of the cabin's maternal lumberyard. The floods had made national news, bringing journalists and photographers from all over the country.

The more we researched, the more amazing photos and facts we uncovered. We quickly learned that if you're genuinely interested in finding out about your home or community, complete strangers are more than willing to help. Our trail eventually led to an elderly gentleman named Milt Lamaster, who, as a small boy, helped his father Frank build our cabin! Many of the photos shown here have never been published before and were generously shared, along with colorful anecdotes, by Milt and other local residents. Turns out, this resilient little town had withstood not one, but four floods (in 1844, 1913, 1922, and 1926), picking itself up, drying itself off, and starting all over again every time.

ABOVE: *The telltale piece of drop siding from the cabin's exterior wall that revealed the name of the original lumberyard.*

143

OPPOSITE: *A phone book advertisement for the Terry Lumber Co. (inset) and the actual lumberyard in Beardstown, Illinois (formerly called Andrews Bros.).*

C-131 ADVISORY BOARD
BEARDSTOWN FLOOD—APRIL, 1922
PHOTO BY CARL A. SWENSON, SPRINGFIELD, ILLINOIS

CITY HALL

C-108 SALVATION ARMY DELIVERING BL
BEARDSTOWN FLOO
PHOTO BY CARL A. SWENSON,

C-732 BOAT FUNERAL
BEARDSTOWN FLOOD—APRIL, 1922

COME HELL AND HIGH WATER

1926

LEFT: *The original cabin builder and owner, Frank Lamaster, with son Milt, row into town during the flood to help evacuate locals. The Lamasters were Beardstown natives and had built three cabins on the outskirts of town just months before the levee broke.*

OPPOSITE: *Scenes from the 1922 Beardstown flood. A very soggy town, indeed.*

145

"Most everyone was told to leave their homes until the town dried up. As I recall, it took months. But ya know, the town was anything but 'dry' during that time, even with Prohibition going on."

—MILT LAMASTER

THE BIRTH OF A TOURIST CABIN

BELOW: *A young Milt with his pet goat (left). Milt with his mother and grandmother thigh-high in the flood waters (right). Unfortunately, his Grandma's house was in town, but she found shelter from the floods at her son's cabin court, along with other locals.*

RIGHT: *Milt Lamaster was just a child when his parents Frank and Iva Dell set up shop. He remembers working alongside his father and a local carpenter to help build the cabins. To this day, his "hammer arm" gets sore just thinking about it! (One of the cabins pictured here is ours, although we don't know which one.)*

The flood was a curse for the town of Beardstown, but it was a blessing for one lucky family that owned a cabin court situated on high ground just a few miles east of town. Frank Lamaster and Iva Dell were melon farmers, tollbooth ticket takers, and the proud proprietors of the recently opened Log Cabin Tourist Camp. Three cabins. Two very entrepreneurial people. And a whole mess of chickens. (The poultry were raised on the front porch of the office, where they would commonly greet the guests who came to pick up a key.)

"I remember when—I couldn't have been more than eight years old—a gent rolled up to the office to ask to rent a cabin for his sweetie who was waiting in the car, and he 'bout jumped out of his skin when he was answered by the mess of chicks that Mom and Dad had on the front porch. We just raised them there. I didn't think a thing of it, but I remember that renter turning on his heels."

MILT LAMASTER

Son of Proprietors

ABOVE *(left to right): The young, handsome entrepreneur Frank Lamaster, and a young Milt posing as a hood ornament on the family car.*

OPPOSITE: *Frank at his second job as the ticket taker at the Beardstown toll bridge. Frank saved these mementos of the job he took pride in—photographs and postcards of the bridge, a ticket stub, a coin—and left them to his son, Milt, who shared them, and his father's story, with me.*

Frank Lamaster was a jack-of-all-trades. Besides establishing Beardstown's first cabin court, he was also a ticket taker at the toll bridge over the Illinois River—a whopping 25 cents for a one-way ticket. He and Iva also tended a large melon patch in the fields near the cabin court. They recognized the opportunity to make some extra cash when Beardstown's famous Watermelon Festival brought thousands of visitors from nearby communities. As a thriving town at the intersection of a major river and several freight train lines, Beardstown was a stopping off point for tugboat captains, train engineers, farmers, and traveling salesmen. It was also the site of the historic Abraham Lincoln Almanac Trial. Add to this the region's legendary catfish, bass fishing, and duck hunting, and this small town had more than its fair share of tourism. By building his cabin court in a rustic log cabin style, Frank was counting on the novelty to appeal to a broad swath of tourists.

Wagon Bridge over Illinois River at Beardstown, Ill.

Made in Germany.

Anderson Drug & Co., Importers & Publishers, Beardstown, Ill.

BEARDSTOWN
BRIDGE
TICKET

3776687

25
EAST

Hon. Wesley Perry,
Mayor.

THE VICE YEARS

LEFT **LEFT** *(clockwise from top left):*
Iva Dell, cabin court proprietor,
shows off her new ride, purchased
with the proceeds of her bustling
business. Two bold, young
lovelies flaunt their stuff down
a main street in Beardstown
during the 1920s. The Goodell
Hotel on Fourth Street was one
of several lodging options within
Beardstown city limits. The main
office building for Frank and Iva's
cabin court when it was new.

RIGHT: *This feisty lady seated*
was also a Beardstownian:
apparently it was fun for the
ladies to ham it up for the camera
by donning mens' hats and
chomping on stogies.

Respectable hotels like The Goodell within the town limits of Beardstown weren't the best choices if you wanted to keep a low profile. Such proper hotels required guests to sign in at the front desk. If you were looking for privacy, you'd head to the Log Cabin Tourist Camp on the outskirts of town. Here, you could pay in advance without registering and check

For a little privacy, you'd head to the outskirts of town, where you could be discreet.

into your own stand-alone cabin, free to disappear into the night when you were done with your business. Although they were intended for the growing tourist trade, many cabin courts—like Frank's—became part of what J. Edgar Hoover later called "camps of crime." With out-of-the-way locations, tourist camps were perfect hideouts for criminals on the run as well as practitioners of the so-called hot pillow trade.

151

LEFT: *This era attracted gin runners, working girls, and gamblers to the cabin court. The little boy on the gin barrel is Milt Lamaster.*

BELOW AND OPPOSITE: *Some of the local Beardstownians during the cabin's heyday.*

MODEL T'S AND DRUNKEN PIGS

As Milt Lamaster tells it, "On a busy night, you could get three or four rentals out of a single cabin, which was obviously more lucrative than a weekend-long rental to a duck hunter." Iva and Frank had not intended to operate their three cabins as a den of iniquity, but just the same, the busier the jezebels, the better for business.

It was a whole new definition of cabin fever.

Milt also recalls another aspect of the era's seedy past: homemade moonshine (aka corn liquor or white lightening), which his father-in-law brewed, as did many of their neighbors.

One afternoon, it appeared the hogs had come down with some sort of rare sickness that left them stumbling dizzily around the cabin court. Before the vet could arrive on the scene, his dad discovered the source of this strange malady: the hogs had helped themselves to the leftovers in the mash barrels!

Reckamp, Beardstown, Ill.

Superior Finish

HORSE NUMBER
1 2 3 4 5 6

WIN
This mutual ticket valid only
if punched by ticket seller,
stamped with date, and
cashed on date sold.
DATE

128645

PRIVATE

A MAKESHIFT HUNT CLUB

By the time the mid 1930s came around, more modern lodging options had become available, and the Log Cabin Tourist Camp had outlived its usefulness. Frank Lamaster picked up his family—and the cabins themselves—and moved them all into town. (Turns out I'm not the only one crazy enough to move a cabin!) The cabin's next life would be as a makeshift hunt club for the locals. After a day of hunting or fishing, the men weren't too anxious to return home. Instead, they'd hole up in the cabin for a few more drinks and several hands of poker. When interviewing some of the older locals to learn about this chapter in the cabin's life, I also found out that both of my grandfathers were likely among those who dropped in for more fraternity after a long day on the river. One older gent recalled a gussied-up mannequin staring out the cabin window; apparently, the guys placed her there as a tribute to the cabin's notorious past!

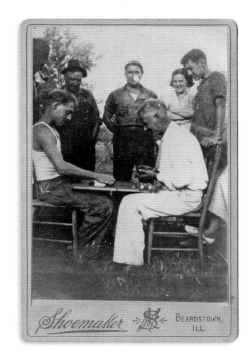

BELOW: *In the decade of duck hunting and gambling, the cabin became a Friday night rod-and-gun club venue for card games. Pictured here are some locals who would partake, including my grandfather, seated on the left.*

155

OPPOSITE: *Photo of my grandfather (seated at left) and another member of the hunt club.*

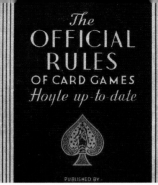

> "I remember when I was young, driving out past the cabins where the guys played cards. One of them propped up a gussied-up mannequin right there in the window of one of the cabins, I guess as a joke or advertising or something. Everybody got a kick out of that."
>
> **GEORGE BUCK, 92, BEARDSTOWNIAN**

MIDDLE AGE:

A TRUCKING COMPANY OFFICE

Years had passed since the now twenty-something-year-old cabins had any legitimate use. They were beginning to show their age. Then along came Art Jones in 1946, fresh from serving his country in World War II. He saw the potential of the run-down cabins: They'd make a perfect office and dispatcher's station for the trucking company he was starting with his brother Louis. Art scooped up two of the cabins and trucked them another mile or so down the road. (These cabins just couldn't stay put!) They were placed on a plot of land next door to my grandmother's house, where they would remain for the next sixty years. The Jones brothers gave the cabins a spit shine and hung their shingle. My mom remembers that every time the phone in the cabin office would ring, it would set off a loud bell that could be heard across the truck yard and throughout the neighborhood. While these two cabins were lucky enough to begin another life in service to Jones Brothers Trucking, the third cabin from the old Log Cabin Tourist Camp has been lost to time.

Home from the war, a soldier becomes an entreprenuer. Meet cabin owner number three.

RIGHT *(clockwise from top left): Art Jones' truck license photo, Art the soldier, Art Jones (right) and his brother Louis, the two cabins on Art's property, Art in one of the original trucks.*

JONES BROS. TRUCKING
Lime Spreading - Fertilizers - Ditching
Phone 216 or 591
Beardstown, Ill.

JONES BROS., Garden St., Beardstown, Ill.

MAY 1949

With my Grandma Harre's house located next door to Jones Bros.Trucking, the cabins provided a backdrop for many family photos of Mom. Likewise, a generation later, my little brother Sam spent many an afternoon sitting on Grandma's porch watching with great interest as the massive trucks rolled in and out. While still in grade school, Sam pestered the Jones brothers into letting him do odd jobs around the truck yard. They started him out as a machine and parts washer, but as Sam earned their respect, he graduated to moving rigs, even though he wasn't old enough for a driver's license and his feet could barely reach the pedals! Over the years, Jones Trucking evolved from hauling feed to digging foundations to hauling coal to providing crane service and equipment delivery. When Art retired, his son A. C. proudly took over the family business. By this time, the business had long since outgrown the little log cabins. When A. C. erected a metal barn with an attached office, the cabins were left to decay. When I finally hatched the scheme of moving and rehabbing one of them, I dispatched Sam to share this idea with his former boss, A. C. Jones.

To this day, the other cabin still sits there, but when A. C. finds the time, he and his wife Becky have discussed moving it out to their land in the country so they can do a little renovation project of their own. Now that I've completed all the research on our own cabin, I like to think a bit of the collective good energy of all the souls who have passed through its door still lives and breathes inside. I like to believe each guest who spends a night there adds a bit more good karma to a cabin that will continue to live and breathe long after me.

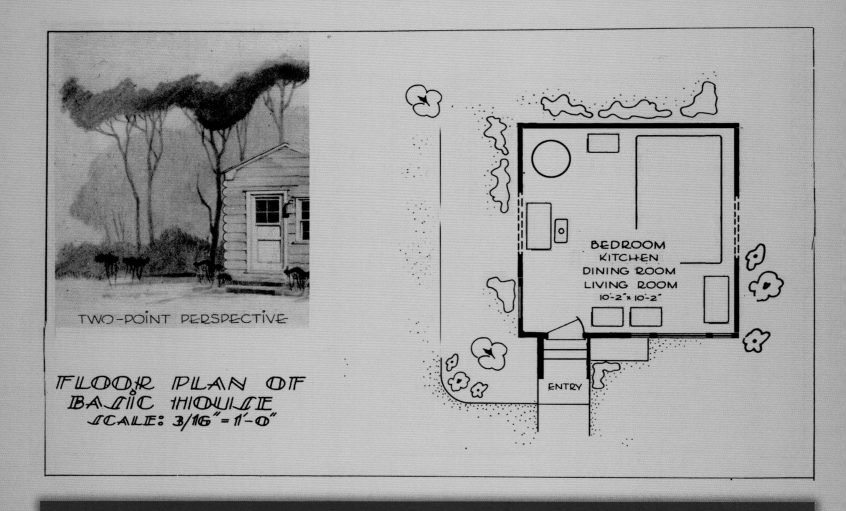

TWO-POINT PERSPECTIVE

FLOOR PLAN OF
BASIC HOUSE
SCALE: 3/16" = 1'-0"

BEDROOM
KITCHEN
DINING ROOM
LIVING ROOM
10'-2" x 10'-2"

ENTRY

A floor plan typical to cabins of the 1920s, with bedroom, dining room, living room, and kitchen all in one small room. Like ours, the kitchen for many cabins was the potbelly stove. Note there is no bathroom. (In case you were wondering, we use the bathroom in a nearby building on our property.)

HOW TO TRACE THE ANCESTRY OF YOUR HOME

While remodeling, many of us have discovered old newspapers shoved behind walls of horsehair plaster and lathing —a telltale sign of the home's origins. But you want to know more. Who built it? And how the heck did this lean-to structure appear in the back—and what's it made out of? Where in the name of all things holy can we find a picture of this place in its "childhood"? Here are a few tips to tracing your home's genealogy. Be careful. Once you start, you may find this treasure hunt addictive and utterly time-consuming.

- Go to your local title office to find out who built it and how many times it changed hands. You'll find the names of prior owners, who, if you're lucky, might have photos of their Great Grandma Maude in front of your house.

- Visit the local historical society. In smaller communities, this venerable institution may run on a $5 annual budget and a host of saintlike volunteers, who are usually as enthusiastic as you are about preserving the past. Always, always make a donation. It's good karma and gets you more help.

- The library offers old newspapers on microfiche, and you may uncover all sorts of things. If you would prefer not to know that three people died in your home from 1885 to 1920, don't look too deep. You'll also find old phonebooks to help identify past owners.

- Plots of survey, which are typically drawings of your property, will point you in the right direction to uncover more documents.

- Building permits can help you piece together the history of when the building was built, added on to, and so on. You can typically find these in the title office.

- Property tax IDs will reveal the names of the builder and various property owners. I found ours in the county seat office of records.

- Place an ad in the local paper, post flyers, and offer a reward for more information.

- Beg. This has proven quite effective for me. That and some home-baked cookies go a long way towards gleaning information from otherwise uninterested locals.

- Hire a researcher.

- eBay is not just for buying and selling anymore. Set your search engine to advanced and enter a broad range of criteria to track down items related to your community. For example, it was common in the early part of the century for photographers to shoot and resell postcards with street scenes.

- Have patience, patience, and more patience. Good luck, and happy hunting.

HOW TO CHARM THE ANSWERMAN INTO TELLING YOU EVERYTHING HE KNOWS

If you are on a quest for information of any kind (in my case the history of a forgotten little log cabin), you should consider seeking out the wisest old souls in town. For us, it was Harold. Harold Tyson (shown opposite, top left) is a saint. And a historian. A local for five decades, he is also the proprietor of the biggest hotspot in town—the barber shop. When he heard what I was looking for, he pulled out his collection of old phonebooks, albums of vintage local postcards, and stacks of personal photos. Arriving to meet me at 7:30 AM, he parked me at his office desk, and I started scanning. And then the customers started filing in. One by one they shared their stories and theories about the cabin's origins. Thirty haircuts later, I had a dozen leads to follow up on.

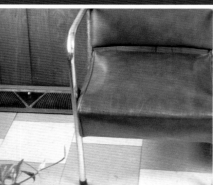

PLAT BOOK of
CASS COUNTY, ILLINOIS

PRICE $3.00 each   Compiled by A. C. HORNBURG, Pu

Cass County Farm Bureau

Virginia, Illinois

1918—1946

My visits to Cass County were primarily focused on the historical society (below) and the local diner where I interviewed Milt Lamaster (left), son of the original builder and owner of the tourist cabin camp that housed our little cabin.

WHEN IS SOMETHING TOO FAR GONE?

An old car, a decrepit piece of furniture, a rusty old tractor, an abandoned cottage? It's not so much about the condition of the thing as it is the ability of a person to believe in it. My dad, Tom Surratt, believed. He had the gift of optimism, seeing the youth—the former self—in everything. He didn't see a worthless geriatric tractor that was too far gone. He imagined his grandson, my nephew Alan, driving that tractor down Main Street one day in the annual Beardstown Fall Fun Festival Parade. He didn't see a rust bucket of a pickup that was beyond hope. Instead, he envisioned a "country limousine" his son Sam would use to drive his bride, Tara, home on their wedding night. Dad's ability to see potential where most others see junk turned out to be a gift passed down to each of his kids, most evident in my brother Sam, who can pretty much bring anything mechanical back to life again. And again.

It's also evident in my sisters Amy, Lisa, and Holly, who married men cut from the same can-do cloth. Men who understand the right combination of ambition, duct tape, and elbow grease makes all things possible. It was a gift he shared with my mom, Kay, who has turned a half dozen condemned properties into homes for low-income families. And it was he who inspired me to see the younger self of an abandoned cabin all but bound for the wrecking ball. I saw a quiet, happy place where Dad could read his books, listen to his grandkids playing, and watch the clouds roll by. Dad didn't make it to see the rebirth of the old cottage. Or to witness Alan, with a grin a mile wide, now old enough to pilot that old International Harvester tractor down Main Street and win best of show for antique restorations. But Dad's ability to believe that a thing is never too far gone lives on in all of us.

RIGHT: *My dad, Tom, in the center. Clockwise from top left: Adam, Holly, Clay, Lisa, Jeff, Tara, Sam, Kay, Rob, Amy, David, me, Alan, Ryan, Heather, and Beth.*

OCT

RESOURCES & CREDITS

LISTEN UP

Some people come to the cabin to write. Some to read. Some to pick a guitar. Some to draw. Some just to sleep. But all to relax. I wanted to fill those walls with a music track that fits the space, sets a mood, and inspires us. So we decided that we needed a cabin playlist. A little country, a little urban, a little obscure, a lot of character. Just like the diverse group of friends we share time with up here.

"Look for the Silver Lining," Chet Baker

"Brown-Eyed Girl," Van Morrison

"Somewhere Over the Rainbow," Israel Kamakawiwo'ole

"King of the Road," Roger Miller

"When We Were Young," The Killers

"Move It on Over," Hank Williams

"Island in the Sun," Weezer

"Feelin' Good," Nina Simone

"Makin' Memories of Us," Keith Urban

"Country Boy," Johnny Cash

"Baby Please Don't Go," Muddy Waters

"Hey Ya!" Outkast

SPEND THE NIGHT

It turns out you can still stay in an early cabin court. Here are a few places that rent out period cabins and cottages. Considering the thousands of cabins that have fallen by the wayside, it's impressive that there are still some standing, let alone still in operation.

Sherwood Court, Eureka Springs, AR
www.sherwoodcourt.com

The Log Cabin Motor Court, Asheville, NC
www.cabinlodging.com

The Pines Cottages, Asheville, NC
www.ashevillepines.com

Vista Court Cabins, Lake Tahoe, NE
www.vistacourtcabins.com

Boulder Motor Court, Twin Mountain, NH
www.bouldermotorcourt.com

Pemi Cabins, Lincoln, NH
www.pemicabins.com

The Patio Motorcourt, Twin Mountain, NH
www.thepatio.com

Hills Motor Court, Alexandra Bay, NY
www.hillsmotorcourt.com

Harbor View Hotel, Lake Geneva, WI
www.lakegenevaharborview.com

Thorp House Inn & Cottages, WI
www.thorphouseinn.com

PHOTOGRAPHY CREDITS

A huge hug of appreciation to all of the friends who donated their lovely photos for inclusion in this book.

All photographs and illustrations shot and created by Tereasa Surratt with the exception of the following:

Vince Cook, page 118, center right; page 170, upper left

Mitch Gordon, page 42, center; page 44-45; page 118, upper right; page 172, bottom left

Matt Gore, page 122, top; page 123, upper left and right, center right; page 128, center right; page 170, center right

David Hernandez, all photos of the author

Tim Hogan, page 118, bottom left

Rob Jillson, page 63, upper right

Jon Oye, page 43

Chris Strong, page 42, right; page 62, left; page 63 all photos except upper right; page 98; page 119, top center; page 172, upper center and right

Björn Wallander, page 120; page 122, bottom left and right and top image; page 123, bottom left; page 124, bottom left and right; pages 126-127, all photos; pages 128-129, all photos except page 128, center right; page 172, upper left

Historical photos courtesy of Milt Lamaster, "Pooch", and Harold Tyson.

ACKNOWLEDGEMENTS

Special thanks to all of those kind souls who contributed their time and efforts to the making of this book, including: the staff at the *Beardstown Gazette*, Cass County Historical Society, Lincoln Courthouse Museum-Beardstown, Tyson Barber Shop, Cass Co. Title Office, Milt McClure Sr., George Buck, and my family.

Jacqueline Deval of Hearst, the reason this little story has grown into an actual book, for her superpower editing skills, sharing her vast experience, amazing guidance, pep talks, sense of humor, and incredible patience with me. Words cannot express my gratitude for making this book happen.

Nancy Soriano, for the great opportunity, your original vision, and the confidence that we could actually do this. You have inspired me, like so many women, more than you know.

Chris Thompson at Sterling, for his design advice, resources, generous time, and fabulous style sense.

Sam Surratt, who gets the T-shirt for "Greatest Brother in the Universe." He inherited the best possible traits from our father; without his resourcefulness, ingenuity, and tolerance of my craziness, none of this would have been possible.

Joe Koehnke, who has helped with nearly every aspect of the resurrection of this cabin; words cannot express our appreciation of yours and Laurie's friendship and help.

Tatertot: it is not possible to thank, love, or appreciate you enough for being you.

Tim Hogan, the most talented, giving person we know. For his collaboration, design skills, late nights, and help. Tim and his team at the Royal Order of Experience Design contributed countless hours executing the design and layout of the book as well as the Web site that accompanies it. Check out their work at www.theroyalorder.com.

William Golden: designer, photographer, rehabber, therapist extraordinaire. William worked with Tim when it occurred to us just how unwieldy this project had become. Check out his work at www.thetwotwo.com.

Milt Lamaster: For sharing his story, photos, time, and wonderful sense of humor during our visits. Milt passed away just before this book went to press. I offer my most sincere gratitude to him and his family.

Donna Charlton-Perrin: For her forever-sunshine optimism, brilliant gift of writing, and being such a great listener and collaborator.

INDEX

ABOUT THE AUTHOR

Tereasa Surratt spent her first seventeen years among the farms of rural Central Illinois, affording her the opportunity for a diverse work background, including watermelon harvester, truck stop waitress, bartender, mural painter, antique dealer, interior designer, and most recently, author.

Her day job is as an advertising creative director, and she has created campaigns for brands such as Dove, Suave, and Sears. In addition to receiving industry awards, her work has garnered attention in national media, including the *Wall Street Journal*, *People*, "Oprah," and "The Tonight Show." She has served as a panelist at industry conferences, juried art shows, and mentored creatives at the Chicago Portfolio School. Tereasa's renovation and interior design projects have been featured in numerous magazines.

She contends that her most valuable skill is as "international flea market haggler." If you travel abroad with her, you can be sure to be dragged to some God-forsaken, obscure, back-alley excuse for a flea market. You might fear for your life, but you will always emerge with the best finds ever.

Tereasa Surratt cannot decide which of her numerous occupations to favor: Art director, roofer, or thrift store junkie? You can follow her ongoing struggle at www.tereasa.com and www.averymodestcottage.com.

Copyright © 2010 by Hearst Communications, Inc.

Cover design: Jon Chaiet
Creative Direction: Tereasa Surratt
Design & layout: Tim Hogan/Aaron Shimer, The Royal Order of Experience Design (www.theroyalorder.com)

Library of Congress Cataloging-in-Publication Data

Surratt, Tereasa.
  A very modest cottage : a 1920s cabin gets a new chance at life / Tereasa Surratt.
    p. cm.
  Includes bibliographical references and index.
  ISBN-13: 978-1-58816-797-2
  ISBN-10: 1-58816-797-6
1. Vacation homes--Wisconsin--Design and construction. 2. Cottages--Illinois--Maintenance and repair.
3. Cottages--Remodeling for other use--Wisconsin. 4. Surratt, Tereasa--Homes and haunts. I. Title.
  TH4835.S87 2010
  690'.873--dc22
                        2009037909

10 9 8 7 6 5 4 3 2 1

Published by Hearst Books
A division of Sterling Publishing Co., Inc.
387 Park Avenue South, New York, NY 10016

Country Living is a registered trademark of Hearst Communications, Inc.

www.countryliving.com

For information about custom editions, special sales, premium and corporate purchases,
please contact Sterling Special Sales Department at 800-805-5489
or specialsales@sterlingpublishing.com.

Distributed in Canada by Sterling Publishing
c/o Canadian Manda Group, 165 Dufferin Street
Toronto, Ontario, Canada M6K 3H6

Distributed in Australia by Capricorn Link (Australia) Pty. Ltd.
P.O. Box 704, Windsor, NSW 2756 Australia

Manufactured in Malaysia

Sterling ISBN 978-1-58816-797-2